Better Than Babylon

A New Vision for Western Culture

Thomas G. Casey, SJ

Paulist Press
New York / Mahwah, NJ

Cover design by Sharyn Banks

Cover images courtesy of Shutterstock.com.: Top, sunset, by Gail Johnson. Center, in purple, by Kellie L. Folkerts. Bottom, background, by Daniel Korzeniewski. Bottom, foreground, image of building, by 1xpert.

Book design by Lynn Else

Library of Congress Cataloging-in-Publication Data
Casey, Thomas G.
    Better than Babylon : a new vision for western culture / Thomas G. Casey.
        p. cm.
    Includes bibliographical references.
    ISBN 978-0-8091-4770-0 (alk. paper) — ISBN 978-1-61643-142-6
1. Christianity and culture. 2. Christian life. I. Title.
    BR115.C8C336 2012
    261—dc23
                                                    2012004645

Published by Paulist Press
997 Macarthur Boulevard
Mahwah, New Jersey 07430

www.paulistpress.com

Printed and bound in the
United States of America

To my godson Thomas David and my sister Anne-Marie

Contents

Preface vii

Introduction: Beginning the Journey 1

1. A New Start 15

2. The Power of the Family..33

3. Teachers Will Shine as Bright as Stars 51

4. Equality for Women......................................63

5. Work to Become Yourself...75

6. It's the Environment, Stupid!.................................86

7. Caring for Our Health 96

8. War Is Awful 105

9. Cultivating the Imagination 117

10. Thinking Outside the Box.................................130

11. Beyond Babylon......................................141

Notes 161

Preface

Theresa's passionate, ideal nature demanded an epic life: what were the many-volumed romances of chivalry and the social conquests of a brilliant girl to her? Her flame quickly burned up that light fuel; and, fed from within, soared after some illimitable satisfaction, some object which would never justify weariness.

George Eliot, *Middlemarch*

I've spent many hours listening to people as they hesitantly break through the surface self to the level of the soul, and then begin to take in the love of God. It is hard for them to arrive at that inner landscape of surprise because they've been in a cycle of self-blame forever. As for religion, they cannot remember how their slow, almost imperceptible journey away from faith began. But somehow they have drifted into a vague distance from God. When they succeed in coming home to themselves and glimpsing their own beauty, something amazing happens: they are blessed with a real compassion for who they are in all their vulnerability, and this compassion carves out a space where they can welcome God into their hearts. It's as though they must first become aware of the marvel of themselves, and only then are they ready to get in touch with the wonder of God. A better self-relationship ushers in a new and nourishing friendship with the One who has always been calling them. This journey inward and upward does not happen overnight: although the heart is only fifteen inches from the head, it can take years to arrive at our emotional core.

What is true at the individual level is also true of our wider society. Western culture is moving so fast that it is hard for us to stop long enough to look compassionately at ourselves and where we are going. This book is an attempt to do just that, and to initiate a two-way conversation between the Gospel and culture. It takes both seriously. Although in some respects Western culture can be a barren spiritual wasteland, shrinking our lives into tired predictability, the act of reflecting on this culture always opens up unsuspected avenues toward new creativity and so liberates our hope. For our part, we Christians can freeze our life-giving message into unhelpful blocks of heady doctrines. Here I try to express the Christian message in an imaginative way, without falling into worn-out clichés. I call on the resources of literature and wisdom to highlight the vitality and fullness of the Good News. The language of Christianity may sometimes sound stale but its message is perennially fresh. Ultimately, it is our Western culture that is too small-minded in its thinking and too miserly in its ambitions. This book stretches our imagination to a size that can harbor our best hopes and give life to our deepest longings.

It was not long ago that Christians were preoccupied with preaching the Gospel to the non-Christian world, which used to be identified with the world outside Western culture. Today we have come to realize that the West is also a mission field, the most challenging of all. As we look back on the missionary past, we see that it was at times sadly interwoven with the impulse of colonial expansion. Today we are blind to the many ways in which Western culture colonizes our minds and sabotages our collective imagination. The cages that confine us are almost invisible, which is why we do not realize we are imprisoned.

I hope this book will be a first step to find freedom in the midst of a confusing and complex culture, a challenge to stop drifting with the prevailing currents, and learn, when necessary, to swim against the tide. If you mindlessly want to let the current take you downriver just because everyone else is traveling in the same direction, you might as well be a corpse: it makes everything fast and painless. But if you want to find the truth, you have to be prepared to swim upstream. It is more difficult, but in the end more rewarding, because there you will find the source, living springs of water.

I am grateful to family and friends, mystics and musicians, poets and prophets, but most of all to God, for helping me see that "there lives the dearest freshness deep down things" (Gerard Manley Hopkins). If you can taste some of this freshness in these pages, I will be more than glad.

Beginning the Journey

> Not all religion is to be found in the church, any more than all knowledge is to be found in the classroom.
>
> Anonymous

One Saturday morning over breakfast I told my parents they might never see me again. I was seventeen years old, had just graduated from high school, and was leaving home forever.

These lines may read like the opening sentences of a confessional novel; in fact, they are true of the author of this book. Today I am shocked by what I said as a naive teenager; back then, I had no idea how callous my declaration sounded. I imagined (wrongly) that being Catholic meant having to get as far away as possible from this world, and I took it as a matter of course that saying extremist things about leaving the world forever was simply part of the package. I fled from the world as though it were the archenemy of my faith. I somehow forgot the obvious fact that Christ took on a human body and entered our human world because he loved both. My lofty approach left me a wounded Catholic for years.

The background may help explain things—it usually does. As a teenager, I had a deep sense of God's presence in my life. I was also pious, but I was afraid to let this show with my peers. They admired me: I had a quick wit and could be the life and soul of the party. But once I got home, I would suddenly change gear, reading devotional books and poring over the lives of the saints. I looked up to the saints because they were so unlike me; they did not care at all about what the world thought: they simply went ahead and loved God to excess. I warmed to their supreme freedom from the tyranny of others' approval or disapproval. I wanted to be free as well. I went to visit monasteries in the Irish countryside and was attracted by the lives of these long-robed men who had withdrawn from the world. They could live their faith in freedom! It was my dream. I began to convince myself that God was calling me to be a monk too.

Although I was deeply spiritual, I was also humanly immature, a desperately self-conscious teenager with a low self-image. I felt I could never be myself before others. I was convinced that if they knew how much God and religion meant to me, they would ridicule me. The last thing I wanted them to think was that I was a religious nut. So I kept my religion to myself, which made me feel like a fraud. I knew I was betraying myself, but most of all God. My life was deeply unsatisfying: the opinions of others swayed me so much that I felt I had lost who I really was. My only hope was to escape this emotional turmoil by entering a monastery. There, I would finally have the opportunity to live my faith unashamedly and in a supportive context where I would not be made fun of or mocked; there, piety would finally be acceptable.

That Saturday morning, breakfast was cornflakes, toast, and a cup of tea, nothing special to suggest the momentous move that was in the air. No Last Supper. No long farewell. Although my parents knew I wanted to go to the monastery, they had presumed it was for a few weeks, just to see what the life of the monk was like from the inside. They had no idea until that Saturday morning that my plan was to go forever. I had no idea how much I was wrenching their hearts.

After breakfast, I picked up a brown leather briefcase into which I had crammed all I was bringing for this ever-lasting journey: toothbrush, paste, pajamas, socks, sandals, trousers, and a Bible. There was no razor blade or shaving foam: I was a baby-faced teenager and had not even begun to grow facial hair.

"At least say goodbye to your brother," my mother pleaded, while my father got the car from the parking garage.

I knew why I didn't want to say goodbye to my brother: I was afraid he would totally disapprove of my decision. Inside I felt I was doing something crazy, and I had a sinking feeling he would confirm my worst fears. As things turned out, I caught my brother off guard. Paul barely had time to wipe the sleep from his eyes before I made my dramatic announcement. He looked thoroughly puzzled, but was nevertheless gracious enough to wish me luck.

An hour later, we drove through the monastery entrance. The car made a loud crunching sound all along the ascending driveway that led up to the main building. My father was driving dead slow now; a funeral hearse would have moved more quickly. I guess he felt I had died and so we had eternity to get there.

My mother looked horrified when she caught sight of the monastery perched on top of a windswept hill. "You could have chosen a pretty monastery, not this ugly monstrosity."

"That's the whole point," I reflected. "If you leave the world, you must really abandon it. No compromises."

My father knocked on the monastery door, and a hooded figure ushered us inside. If anything, the interior of the monastery looked even more austere than its façade, without the least hint of warmth or welcome. The monk pointed us to a small guestroom and went off in search of the abbot. My mother was crying so much the room was beginning to flood, while my father looked like he was resigned to drowning.

After what seemed like an age, the abbot finally arrived. A feeling of panic overcame me when I saw him: this was not the man who had been running the monastery two months before, the kindly and indulgent figure who had given in to my youthful persistence. I remembered that avuncular figure with great fondness: "You're a bit too fresh-faced and wet behind the ears for my liking," he had said, before adding, "but God has his own time and we must respect it."

The new abbot could not have been more dissimilar from the previous one. He had a tough, no-nonsense style. He cast a quick glance at my bewildered father, my grieving mother, and the terribly innocent child sitting between them. He made up his mind at that moment.

"Father Abbot," my mother cried. "I've tried talking to him, but he won't listen to sense or reason. He's got it into his head and that's that. He's coming here forever."

"Well, then, he'll just have to get it out of his head, won't he, Mrs. Casey?" the abbot immediately replied. He looked at me for a moment and continued, "We certainly can't accept a mere child of seventeen for life."

"Glory be to God!" my mother cried. "I knew it, I knew it all along." I cringed at this sudden and belated revelation of maternal omniscience.

"Tom could certainly spend a few weeks here and see how we live our lives, but as for joining on a permanent basis," he added, looking at me firmly, "that's not a decision that can be lightly taken without a long process of prayer and direction."

"Oh, let him stay here a good month. It will sort him out," said my mother. She turned to me and whispered loudly enough for all to hear, "That will soon cure you of your monastic urges."

I soon discovered that my mother was right, much as I hated to admit it. The monastery was not the romantic life I imagined. I did not spend my days in ecstatic prayer but shoveling manure, planting trees, and mending fences. When I was not doing manual work with the monks, we gathered in the chapel to pray, facing each other in two choirs and reciting the psalms aloud. I enjoyed the rhythm and reverence of these prayers, but the whole formula did not bring me the happiness I felt was missing from my life. I had thought I would magically connect with bliss once I crossed the monastic threshold. Instead, I discovered a place not so different from the world I had just left, with the same kinds of people, the same foibles and idiosyncrasies. There were a few saints inside, but there were also ordinary men who were a lot like I was. Although I escaped the external noise and clutter, I was the same Tom inside, full of the noise of self-disapproval.

In sum, I had fled a world I thought was bereft of God in order to find a God I presumed to be totally separate from the world. I had a most "un-Catholic" way of seeing the world, as though it were completely profane, a realm from which God had fled. Despite actively participating in the sacramental life of the Church—as a teenager I went to Mass practically every day—I had a non-sacramental view of the universe: I imagined God was far removed from the world and didn't particularly like it. It had never dawned upon me that God had created the world in love, and had passionately left clues to the fact everywhere. I had not come to see how the persons and events of my daily life were already signs of God, evoking God's presence in deep and mysterious ways. I had focused on God's transcendence, on

God's unlikeness to us, but had failed to balance this distant way of seeing things with a warmer perspective that emphasizes God's immanence and similarity to us.

I had wanted to highlight for myself how unlike me God was; I had failed to see how like us all God truly is. In fact, God lurked in my longings and stood knocking at the door of my heart while I was wasting my time smashing through upper-floor windows that did not lead anywhere worthwhile. I did not companion myself in my joys, yet had I paid compassionate attention to these stirrings of happiness I would have heard in them the symphony of God's own infinite joy. Had I recognized the love in my heart for what it was, I would have seen how God was at work in this love. God was intimately involved in my life, but I was sadly ignorant of the riches inside me. My world was entwined with God, but I had created an unreal alternative and entwined myself around it. To find God, I did not have to leave the world forever; instead I needed to come home to the world (and to myself), and God would be there waiting for me.

What did my brief flirtation with monasticism teach me? A lesson that took me years to learn: the people in my world and the things that happen in my life already speak to me of God. They are signs of God, they are avenues to God. Through them, God becomes present to me. Being a Christian does not come at the price of hating the world. God created the world, and hating it ultimately betrays a deep resentment against God.

But if hatred of the world is fundamentally wrong, innocuous acceptance is not a realistic stance either. The world is a combination of shadow and light. The art is to live by the light and not get sucked in by the darkness. When it comes to this world that forms us, the skill is to avoid the extremes of accepting it completely and rejecting it outright. It is the skill of being in the world and yet not of it.

The myth of Babylon captures well the ambivalence of our world. Babylon has a double identity: it is both a real city of antiquity and a mythical place. Over two and a half thousand years ago, for a short period of time, Babylon, with its hanging gardens and ziggurat of Marduk, was one of the most glorious cities on earth. Today, all that remains of its ancient splendor is a mound of ruins an hour's drive south of Baghdad, Iraq. For centuries, the symbolic Babylon from the Bible's Book of Revelation has exerted a powerful pull on the Western artistic and religious imagination. Chapters 17 and 18 of the Book of Revelation portray it as a powerful, wealthy, and wicked place, doomed to destruction. Like the real Babylon, its glory is short-lived.

Today, any one of us can have hundreds of friends on Facebook and still feel terribly alone. This loneliness is a part of *our* Babylon, our globalized superficiality, where online friendships and text messages fail to satisfy our deep thirst for communion. Our Babylon is never switched off: consumerist society offers a continuous spectacle, but never truly switches us on, like the thousand television channels we flick through, only to find nothing worth watching. Our Babylon is the seductiveness that leads us to mistake glamor for beauty, like the pretty face on the cover of a fashion magazine that momentarily catches our eye and is just as quickly forgotten. This Babylon of ours is so alluring that we do not notice how it anesthetizes our spirit. But it is really only half a life, so shriveled and shrunken that it deadens the self.

The poet Rilke once remarked that the great French artist Cézanne did not paint things as he wanted to see them, but as they were. He was not seduced by Babylon, so to speak, but sought to see what was there as it truly was. For the same reason, Van Gogh commented that modern artists are great thinkers, for they go beyond appearances to reach the very heart of reality. They do not impose their own ideas on things, but bow before the wonder of all that is.

Although appearances should not be confused with reality, they are nevertheless important, because they can lead us to something real. Here is a concrete example: in the United States today, there are over 22 million ex-Catholics, a figure of staggering proportions. This "appearance," this statistic, is telling us something, but what? Half of those who have left the Catholic Church have joined various Protestant Churches. What are their reasons for moving to another denomination? The abuse scandals? Church teaching on birth control or divorce? These are certainly factors, but things are not always as they appear, for these issues, although important, are not their principal concerns. The overriding reason given for leaving the Catholic Church—by a whopping 71 percent of respondents in the Pew Forum Survey—is that their spiritual needs were not being met by the Catholic Church. They are looking for sustained spiritual nourishment, and they feel Catholicism is only giving them junk food.

We priests are partially to blame for this sorry state of affairs. We have not been bright torches, but flickering flames; we have not been on fire with love, but lukewarm; we have not breathed life, but choked people spiritually. Where they have thirsted, we have failed to give them nourishing water. Mahatma Gandhi said he liked Christ, but not Christians, for he could not see a family resemblance. Christianity will be liberated when we priests free ourselves from our spiritually comatose state, and wake up from our apathy and indifference. Only then will people truly see Christ in us. We need to go back to the basics: living simple and humble lives, praying, reading the Gospel, celebrating the Mass with devotion, loving God and our neighbor.

The scandal of clerical sex abuse has shown how far away from the basics some priests have gone. Even though abuse has involved no more than 4 percent of priests, any percentage involved in abuse is sickening. Innocent children have been scarred for life. All right-minded priests feel ashamed of what a small minority of priests has done. These criminal priests abused their power. Babylon is a symbol of power that works against God and against love, attacking goodness and wounding the innocent. Although dioceses around the world are apologizing to victims, reporting accusations, removing accused priests from ministry, and putting child protection programs into place, even the best policies cannot undo the damage done. The victims of abuse will never be the same again. Babylon has wreaked its havoc.

In this age when priests have fallen from the pedestals upon which they were once elevated, I find the lyrics of Leonard Cohen's 1984 song "Hallelujah" returning again and again to my mind. It is a song that took Cohen five years to write, and it was a classic slow-burner: it received scant attention when it was first released in the eighties, but has now achieved legendary status, thanks to countless cover versions and performances. This gospel-like waltz comes to eighty verses, though only a handful are ever sung in most recordings and performances. Cohen, a Canadian singer-songwriter, has said that "Hallelujah" is about the drama of each human life, a drama with its ups and downs, its victory and losses. There are no neat answers or glib solutions to the messiness of a typical human story, and that is why all the song promises are occasional moments of grace when we manage to affirm some sense of meaning despite all the confusion, moments when we proclaim, "Hallelujah! Blessed is the name."

The words of the song mix together the fall of Samson and that of King David: Samson loses his legendary strength when his hair is cut, and David loses his moral authority when he seduces Bathsheba and has her husband killed. These two men, blessed with enormous gifts and stupendous power, are brought low to the dust. Samson becomes blind and weak; David loses the child he has conceived with Bathsheba, and from now on, his firm grip on power will slowly unravel. Both men's stories are evoked in the haunting opening verses of "Hallelujah." Everything had been so easy. It was all laid out before them, but now they find themselves in a dark and unknown place. Love is no longer straightforward: "It's a cold and it's a broken Hallelujah."

All priests feel implicated by the guilt of a few priests. The wounds remain open, and the victims are still bleeding. When we priests look at ourselves collectively, we cannot point to any great virtues of which we are proud. We can only stand before our Creator with empty hands, as Cohen's song puts it, "with nothing on my tongue but Hallelujah." There is nothing triumphant about the Hallelujah we sing; it gives voice only to God's greatness—and to our thoroughgoing fragility.

The song "Hallelujah" reminds us that it is not easy to get beyond Babylon. We cannot simply turn on the lights and extinguish the darkness; we cannot blithely rush forward toward a Hollywood, happily-ever-after ending. Things must run their course. "Hallelujah" respects the slow rhythm of healing even as it gently nudges us forward on our quest. Its lyrics speak with authority rather than power. They invite a response. This response is a yes that is as fragile as we are. It is a yes that has to be chosen and re-chosen in the face of the perennial temptation to say no.

This book is an invitation to go beyond Babylon, to break free of those aspects of Western culture that imprison us, not literally, but through reductive images of happiness and fulfillment. It is a call to reject all those subtle forms of enslavement that stop us from seeing the larger picture, all those superficial images that conspire to prevent us from touching the soul of things. As a teenager, I had a tiny image of God and the world. Fleeing to a monastery would not have freed me; instead it was a recipe for imprisoning me even more securely within a narrow-minded picture of things. This book takes key issues in our culture—women, the family, education, work, the environment, and war and peace—and goes beyond habitual ways of looking at them. We can easily get stuck in one way of seeing things, and presume this is the only way to see. We can mistake a single black-and-white picture for the kaleidoscopic richness of reality.

For now, let me refer to just one example of expanding our worldview, an example from the next chapter, which is about the way Christians relate to Jews. Why did I include a topic like this when there are so many other important questions clamoring for our attention? Fundamentally because Judaism is an unvisited layer of the Christian story, and visiting this forgotten level of our faith is necessary in order to uncover the richness of who we really are. In addition, we have little idea of who Jews are. We only know that we have badly misrepresented these close, yet little-known brothers and sisters over the course of the centuries. A blessing is bestowed on all of us who learn to relate to the Jewish people in a way that treats them with dignity and respect; it is a blessing that is mediated through Abraham and his descendants: "In you all the families of the earth shall be blessed" (Gen 12:3). By learning from our mistakes and by finding a more graced way of relating to Jews, we Christians can also discover a new and better model for relating to all other faiths and races. We share a sacred book with observant Jews, but with all faiths we share the book of creation, the sacredness of a world where we can find signs of God's love for everyone.

The blessing of the imagination opens us up to spheres of life beyond the cautionary confines of our being. It blesses us with a bigger and better life. A liberated imagination already sees what is not yet there. It sees how things could be, sees that they need not be like they are now, that there is a way out of our difficulties. This kind of imagining awakens hope within us. But we cannot expect to imagine a better future on our own. It is only when we share with others, when we combine our imagination with theirs, that we truly escape from the prison of the moment and expand our possibilities. Hope is not something that we can dig out in desperation from our own heart and then magically bring forth into the world in one last act of bluster and audacity. The truth is that we hope best when we lean on others. Hope is not a solitary creation. Hope really happens in relationship, whether with other human beings or with God.

Babylon blocks our access to the door of possibility. Babylon impoverishes us, limiting what we can say and imagine. It cuts us off from many enriching dimensions of life. By so doing, it wounds an essential part of our humanity: the invisible core. At the core of our being is the vital principle called the soul: invisible, intelligent, free, and immortal. This invisible gem gives us the daring and the ability to love without limits. But Babylon wants to constrict us and tie us down. It does not want us to enter an open-ended world where we can risk becoming who we really are and so, as a substitute, offers us a thousand different brand-names to choose from. The choices that Babylon sets before us are risk-free and guarantee instant satisfaction. Living within the limits of Babylon seems prudent and sensible:

Why not take what's there in front of us when we can get it? After all, the future is unknown and invisible. We cannot even see our own thoughts. Babylon offers a safe and circumscribed set of satisfactions, and focuses our attention on small and short-term goals. But God has bigger hopes for us than Babylon could ever entertain. God wants to offer us something we do not yet have, something we do not even know we don't possess. An undreamt-of gift, but wrapped in a gentle invitation card. As the prophet Elijah discovered in the First Book of Kings, God is not in the gale-force winds, the great earthquakes, or the raging fires. God is in the gentle breeze, the still, small, inviting voice that is so close to silence. Because of the din of Babylon, we often do not hear this whispering voice reverberate in our hearts.

But whoever has ears can hear, and this book is an invitation to hope. Hope acknowledges that we are seeking something we do not yet possess. Hope also admits that we are aiming for something that is not easy to achieve. But hope nevertheless boldly believes that we can get there, that this future, although difficult, is thoroughly possible. There is a way out. Babylon, comfortable as it may be, need not be our lasting prison. The world of possibility is much vaster than we have dared imagine. This truth can set us free.

CHAPTER ONE

A New Start

Judaism formed our ideas of God and man, of sanctity, justice, and love: love of God, family, nation, and mankind.

David Gelernter, *Judaism: A Way of Being*

Jerusalem has its very own version of Dublin's Grafton Street, a pedestrian zone in the heart of the city, filled with souvenir shops and sidewalk cafés, where street musicians entertain passers-by each day. When I was younger and more brazen, I headed down there one Saturday evening with my guitar in hand. The sun had just gone down, ending the Jewish Sabbath, the stores were open again, and young people were beginning to throng this street that had been practically deserted since the evening before. I stood at a good vantage point where a small side street ran off Ben Yehuda Street, and went through my repertoire of Beatles' songs. To my delight, people kept dropping shekels into my open guitar case. At one point an Orthodox man and his young son, taking an evening stroll, stopped to listen. They were both dressed in black suits and white shirts, with wide-brimmed hats on their heads. The father sported a long beard. Each of them had ringlets and curls of hair pushed forward over their ears. The little boy smiled with childlike joy as I sang "Yellow Submarine." When I had finished, his father said, "Brother, play something in Hebrew!"

I was flattered—and also strangely touched—that he mistook me for a fellow Jew. I also immediately began to panic, because I did not know any song in his native language. But suddenly I had a flash of inspiration. There was one Hebrew tune I knew, primarily because it comprised only three words. I launched into the famous folk song *"Havenu Shalom Aleichem."* My own enthusiasm grew as I repeatedly sang the familiar words, and when I finished it with a flourish, both father and son beamed with delight. It was a dreamlike and charmed moment, for there was an instantaneous connection. Although it lasted only an instant, for that brief time there was a real and living bond between us. We had transcended the customary boundaries that divide people into tidy and distinct categories. Something unheard and unseen had united us through the melody we had just shared.

I was deeply grateful to be the catalyst of that joyous moment in their lives, because of all that I and my ancestors have received from the Jews. Christianity has many unacknowledged Jewish features, and perhaps if it owned up to them more, it might become more spiritually nourishing and more alive. In the past, Christianity often based its identity upon the rejection of Judaism, or upon the claim that God completely disinherited the Jews and gave Christians everything in their place. But happily we are coming to a more balanced and mature assessment today. We no longer feel the need to assert our Christian identity at the price of the repudiation of the Jews. There is no doubt that Jews and Christians have different ways of living; but it is also true that we Christians are indebted to the Jewish people for how we have learned to live.

Let's look at the heart of Christianity, at Jesus himself. When Jesus returned to his hometown of Nazareth in chapter 4 of Saint Luke's Gospel, he went to the synagogue. It was the Sabbath. He was given the scroll of the prophet Isaiah. Now, this text was not any old text. The Hebrew of this passage is of an extremely sophisticated kind, somewhat like the English in a Shakespearian play. In fact, reading this passage aloud is like trying to recite the famous "To be, or not to be" soliloquy from *Hamlet*. Many actors aspire to reading Hamlet's marvelous speech, and many are terrified of even attempting this feat, because it is much easier to get this soliloquy wrong than right.

Something else to bear in mind about the passage from Isaiah is that the Hebrew text Jesus was given had no vowels and no punctuation. There were no comfortable spaces between the words to facilitate reading it; in fact, one word ran straight into the next. All this makes Jesus' impeccable delivery and rendition of this passage even more extraordinary:

> He unrolled the scroll and found the place where it was written:
>
> "The Spirit of the Lord is upon me,
>   because he has anointed me to bring good news to
>   the poor.
> He has sent me to proclaim release to the captives
>   and recovery of sight to the blind,
>   to let the oppressed go free,
> to proclaim the year of the Lord's favor."
>
> And he rolled up the scroll, gave it back to the attendant, and sat down. The eyes of all in the

> synagogue were fixed on him. Then he began to
> say to them, "Today this scripture has been ful-
> filled in your hearing." All spoke well of him and
> were amazed at the gracious words that came
> from his mouth. (Luke 4:17–22)

Jesus spoke so fluently and authoritatively that his words
were full of life and power. He did not hesitate for a
moment; he did not trip or stumble over his lines. It was
obvious that he was completely at home with the Hebrew
Scriptures, and with speaking in a synagogue. He was in his
natural element: the religion and world of Judaism. This was
the world he had grown up in, the milieu to which he
belonged.

Although Christians are beginning to see the
Jewishness of Jesus more clearly today, for Jews the figure of
Jesus has often symbolized everything that is most anti-
Jewish in the Christian faith. Until relatively recently, they
instinctively associated him with the persecution and violence they have experienced at the hands of Christians over
the centuries. Jesus, the door to salvation for Christians, has
been a stumbling block for the Jews.

The newly developing relationship between Christians
and Jews is doing much to change this negative Jewish
image of Jesus. He is no longer seen by so many Jews as a
symbol of intolerance and persecution. But Jewish people
still find the figure of Jesus disturbing for another reason.
Ironically, it is the same reason that the Christian message
proclaims him as so appealing: his crucifixion. For
Christians, the crucifixion of Jesus is the source of new life
for all; for the Jewish people, this same crucifixion is an
image of death and ritual impurity. The Jewish faith cele-
brates life in all its fullness, and the figure of the crucified

Jesus appears to be the antithesis of everything positive that it stands for.

I instinctively see the cross in a completely different way, as something reassuring and life-giving. I have grown up seeing the cross everywhere: at home, school, church, public buildings, and art galleries—and hanging around people's necks. Each time I pray, I make the Sign of the Cross. It takes a real effort on my part even to begin to grasp how harsh and strange is the death symbolized by this image, and how challenging it is to reconcile this image of Jesus' utter abandonment on the cross with the enormous love of his Father for him. The crucifixion of Jesus will never unsettle me in the way it unsettles my Jewish friends. But their unease does help me refrain from domesticating the strangeness of the cross; their sense of shock at least reawakens the challenge of the cross for me, and that is a salutary thing.

In a similar way, the fact that Jesus followed the Jewish practices of his time shows me that his humanity is not as familiar as I once thought it was. There are many aspects of his culture and religious practices of which I am ignorant. But at the same time, just because Jesus was Jewish, I am not suggesting that all Christians should convert to Judaism. Jesus claimed to be faithful to Judaism, yet he spoke about the Jewish faith in a way that his Jewish contemporaries did not always agree on. He also made a huge claim about himself—that he was the Messiah, the Son of God. This is a claim that Christians believe and Jews reject. So Jesus did not have a cozy and comfortable relationship with the Jewish world of his time.

But for all that, we cannot simply dismiss the Jewishness of Jesus. If Christians want to be like Jesus, true God and true man, they need to know more about the human Jesus of Nazareth as well as the divine Son of God: for instance, the fact that he went to synagogue, observed the rules of the Sabbath, and celebrated the Jewish feasts. It is amazing how effortlessly we forget that Jesus never read the New Testament (which, of course, was not written during his lifetime), but on the other hand he was thoroughly familiar with the Hebrew Scriptures. Since Jesus was Jewish and we Christians follow Jesus, we could benefit from knowing this Jewish side of him better.

The following facts should be obvious, but many Christians overlook them: Jesus was Jewish because he was born of a Jewish mother. His foster father, Joseph, was Jewish as well. His childhood friends, his disciples, the people to whom as a rule he preached were all Jewish. He taught in the synagogue, and he went to the Temple in Jerusalem for the pilgrimage festivals and also for Passover. So how come Christians have overlooked something so obvious? One reason is that Jesus spent a lot of time arguing with certain Jews. In one way, the fact that Jesus was involved in so many arguments should not surprise us: after all, David Ben Gurion, the first prime minister of Israel, once remarked that for every two Jews, there are at least three opinions. Jews like arguing, and Jesus was a Jew; therefore, it is likely that Jesus had no qualms about entering into lively discussions.

It is not only because of these arguments that we forget Jesus was Jewish. It is also because of the people with whom he was arguing. Jesus was at odds with certain significant Jewish figures of his time. For instance, he argued a lot with the Pharisees and the Sadducees. We can easily draw the wrong conclusion. Since Jesus was so often at loggerheads with these two groups, especially the Pharisees, we imagine he was against Judaism as such. But the fact that he argued with certain Jewish groups like the Pharisees or Sadducees, did not mean he was anti-Jewish, or against his own people. Jesus did not hate the people from whom he came and to which he belonged. He loved his fellow Jews and he loved the religion of his people. Recall that wonderful passage from the fourth chapter of Luke that I just quoted. Jesus returned to the synagogue in his hometown of Nazareth and spoke with great eloquence and charismatic authority about fulfilling the words from Isaiah that he had just read aloud. Yet despite the authority that flowed from him, never once during his ministry did Jesus use his authority to change even a single statute or rule from the Pentateuch, the first five books of the Bible. He certainly explained texts and unlocked their spirit and meaning. But he never took it upon himself to alter them.

In fact, Jesus solemnly declared: "Do not think that I have come to abolish the law or the prophets; I have come not to abolish but to fulfill. For truly I tell you, until heaven and earth pass away, not one letter, not one stroke of a letter, will pass from the law until all is accomplished" (Matt 5:17–18). Jesus' actions confirmed his words. Although certain Pharisees accused him of breaking the Law, Jesus never contravened any significant aspect of the Law. In everything that was important, he followed the Law faithfully. Jesus may have expanded the Law, but he did not reject it. Theophylact of Bulgaria, the eleventh-century bishop and interpreter of the Bible, used a striking image to show what Jesus did with the Law: he compared Jesus to an artist who colored in the outlines of a painting.

Perhaps the major reason Christians have forgotten that Jesus is Jewish is because of the way Christianity itself developed. To the early Christians, it was so obvious that Jesus was Jewish that they did not speak much about this fact. Christianity started out as a movement within Judaism, the Jesus movement. The first Christians believed in Jesus, but they still went to the synagogue, practiced circumcision, and followed Jewish dietary laws. At first, they did not even bother much about sharing the Good News with non-Jews, because they presumed the message was mainly directed toward the Jewish people. It was only after Peter, the leader of the early Church, had a vision, described in Acts 10, that he took in the reality that God accepted people from every nation, and not only the Jews. Despite their strong Jewish identity, the first Christians were not totally absorbed into the Judaism of their time: they proclaimed that Jesus was the Messiah and that God had raised him from the dead, and they met in small groups to pray and worship together. By the year AD 64, it was obvious to outsiders that Christians were different from Jews. So much so that the Emperor Nero targeted Christians for persecution (and did not confuse them with Jews), blaming the followers of this new faith for the devastating fire that broke out in Rome that year. Nero had Christians tortured, burned, thrown to the dogs, and crucified.

Over time, Christianity distinguished itself more and more from Judaism. Circumcision was no longer required, and Christians did not have to keep kosher. Scholars diverge widely on when the definitive split between Christianity and Judaism took place and why exactly it occurred. In any event, with the passage of time, Jesus was no longer thought of as a Jew, but primarily as the founder of Christianity. This was a big change. Of course Jesus was a Jew, but this fact was not something that Christians were particularly keen to highlight. They wanted to show they were *not* Jews, not only because Jews were not looked on favorably in the Roman world, but above all because they wanted to mark themselves as the real successors of everything the Hebrew Bible had said and promised. Talking too much about the Jewishness of Jesus would have only confused things in people's minds. Christians share this tendency today. When we look back at Jesus, we see the Son of God as the founder of Christianity, and not as someone who was also faithful to Judaism.

Not only have we Christians ignored the fact that Jesus was Jewish; we have also forgotten how Jewish our own roots are as a result. In fact, for almost 2,000 years, we Christians have had a major blind spot when it comes to Jews. It was only in the wake of the Holocaust and the creation of the State of Israel that the Christian Churches finally began to invest energy into developing a better way of relating to Jews. It was thanks to the determination and energy of Pope John XXIII that Catholicism finally began to rethink its relationship with Judaism. In fact, on the Catholic side, the story of the new relationship with Judaism in the twentieth century is to a large extent the story of two popes—John XXIII and John Paul II—who began to reach out to the Jewish people long before they were ever elevated to the throne of Saint Peter.

Years before he became Pope John XXIII, Angelo Giuseppe Roncalli was based in Istanbul as papal nuncio of the Holy See to Turkey and Greece. According to certain estimates, Roncalli's intervention during World War II helped tens of thousands of Jews flee persecution in Nazi-occupied Europe and get safe passage to Palestine.

I like to picture Roncalli on a warm evening in Istanbul, perhaps in 1942. The sun is setting. Dressed in black, this smiling, stocky man with the friendly face is looking down on the Bosporus Strait beneath him. Flocks of seagulls fly in the wake of the fishing boats and ferries that navigate their way along this channel of water dividing Europe from Asia. Roncalli says a short prayer and breathes a long sigh of relief, because he knows that in the midst of this busy boat traffic, there is one fishing vessel crammed with Jewish refugees headed for Palestine, escaping from the horrors of Nazi persecution. God's providence has brought this man from a modest family of farmworkers near Bergamo, in northern Italy, to Istanbul at this dark time in history. He has never for a moment seen himself as a hero. He is just doing his best to help the Jewish people. But by helping the Jews at this time and in this place, Roncalli becomes a hero.

Angelo Giuseppe Roncalli became Pope John XXIII in 1958. Soon after becoming the leader of the Roman Catholic Church, he eliminated the words *perfidus* (non-believing) and *perfidia judaica* from the Good Friday prayers. In October 1960, John XXIII welcomed a Jewish delegation to the Vatican, saying, "I am Joseph, your brother!" The words are from the famous story in Genesis: Joseph, the favorite son of Jacob, is sold into slavery in Egypt. Later, when his family comes upon hard times, his brothers travel to Egypt to get grain. They meet Joseph but do not recognize him. After questioning them, Joseph reveals who he is, crying out, "I am your brother, Joseph" (Gen 45:4). When Pope John XXIII quoted these very words, did he mean that Christianity, like Joseph, was finally becoming reconciled with its "older brothers," the Jews? Was he suggesting that the Church, like Joseph in Egypt, having lived far away from its roots in Judaism, was now restoring the familial bond? Perhaps some of these issues were in his mind, but in the remarks that followed, he revealed above all what he meant. John XXIII continued by saying that the differences between Christians and Jews do not remove their common brotherhood that comes from having the one Father.

In 1960, Pope John XXIII gave the German Jesuit Cardinal Augustin Bea the task of drawing up a draft document on the relationship between the Church and the Jewish people. Pope John XXIII realized that Augustin Bea was a man of outstanding qualities. That is why he relied on Bea's courage, intelligence, and diplomatic gifts to draft a document for Vatican II on the Church's relations with Judaism—and to push it through. Augustin Bea had not anticipated becoming a cardinal or playing such a significant role in the new history between the Church and the Jewish people. In 1956, on the occasion of his seventy-fifth birthday, Augustin Bea looked back over his life and commented that God had guided him along paths he had never expected, and had made something of him that he had never even imagined.

Bea possibly thought in 1956 that he was coming to the end of his days, but luckily he was wrong: his best years were yet to come (by the way, his later life offers an encouraging lesson to all those who think they are too old to make a difference). When Pope John XXIII gave him the red hat in 1959, Bea told the pope that he would use the authority and responsibility conferred on him by the office of cardinal to work above all for the noble goal of reestablishing unity between Christians. On meeting Cardinal Bea in 1960, W. A. Visser 't Hooft, general secretary of the World Council of Churches, remarked that Bea had not only read and studied the books of the Hebrew Bible, but had also absorbed their wisdom.

Cardinal Bea was the principal architect of the Vatican II declaration *Nostra Aetate* ("In our times"), on the relation of the Church to non-Christian religions. After long and lively discussions and debates among the council fathers, *Nostra Aetate* was voted into being on October 28, 1965. The core of this document is the section on Judaism. It immediately created a new and positive paradigm for relations between the Catholic Church and the Jewish faith. Pope John XXIII did not live to enjoy this milestone; he died two years before it was promulgated. But the new pope, Paul VI, was so excited by *Nostra Aetate* that he immediately declared it was proof that the Church was alive, thinking, and growing.

Overnight, Catholic teaching about the Jewish people shifted from being a teaching of disapproval and even censure to being a teaching of respect and love. It was truly a sea change, a momentous shift in mentality.

Nostra Aetate declared that there is a special spiritual bond between the Catholic Church and the Jewish people. It stated clearly that God loves the Jews. It encouraged Catholics to discover and cherish their Jewish heritage. It reminded Catholics that Jesus and the first disciples were Jewish, and that the Church itself is rooted in Judaism. It urged Christians not to put the blame for Jesus' death on all the Jews of Jesus' time or on the Jews of today. It resolutely condemned all forms of anti-Semitism. It explained that the destiny of the Church would always be interwoven with that of the Jewish people.

Nostra Aetate is a remarkable—and terribly overdue—achievement of Catholicism. It is so revolutionary (in a positive and constructive way), going against centuries of suspicion and prejudice, that its implications have not yet been fully absorbed by Catholics. We (and I include clergy as well as laypeople here) are only beginning to come to grips with this truly prophetic document.

Unfortunately, it is also an achievement about which millions of Christians are partially or completely unaware.

Many do not realize that Christianity has articulated a new and positive stance toward Judaism. *Nostra Aetate* appeared toward the end of the Second Vatican Council in 1965. But the 1960s are now a distant memory for the majority of Catholics in the world. One priest gave a questionnaire to his class, asking students to explain what Vatican II was. One young man wrote down in response, "The pope's summer home"! And even though *Nostra Aetate* is freely available on the Internet, you would almost think it was classified material because most ordinary Catholics have no idea that a revolution has taken place in Christian-Jewish relations.

Although one pope had the wonderful idea of creating this document that represented an astonishing transformation in the received Christian view of Judaism, it fell to a more recent pope to build on this marvelous platform and make even further strides forward: John Paul II.

In early 1945, a thirteen-year-old Jewish girl came out of a Nazi labor camp in Czestochowa, Poland. With no food in her stomach and hardly any flesh on her bones, she sat down exhausted in the corner of a train station, still clothed in the striped uniform of a prisoner. It was the middle of the Polish winter. The weather was freezing, the wind biting cold. These were the final months of a long and senseless war, and people were weary from their own suffering. No one noticed the little, emaciated girl huddled in the corner.

No one, except for a young seminarian. He approached her, struck up a conversation, and helped her. His name was Karol Wojtyla. Thanks to his kindness, she survived. Edith Zierer later recalled: "I remember perfectly well. I was there, I was a thirteen-year-old girl, alone, sick, and weak. I had spent three years in a German concentration camp at the point of death. And, like an angel, Karol Wojtyla saved my life; like a dream from heaven: he gave me something to drink and eat and then carried me on his back some four kilometers in the snow, before catching the train to safety."[1]

For many years, Edith kept this story to herself. Then in 1978, when Karol Wojtyla was elected pope, she knew she simply had to tell people about it. On March 23, 2000, forty-five years after being rescued by this young seminarian, she had the opportunity to thank him personally when they met in the Yad Vashem Museum in Jerusalem.

Pope John Paul II's visit to the Holy Land was the high point of the Jubilee Year 2000 and also one of the high points of his whole papacy. On the same day that Pope John Paul II met Edith Zierer, he also listened to an address by the Israeli prime minister Ehud Barak, who remarked that John Paul II had felt the sufferings of the Jewish people as though they were his own sufferings. Barak also praised him for continuing the great path opened up by Pope John XXIII: "As you wrote to your Jewish childhood friend, you felt, in some sense, as if you yourself experienced the fate of Polish Jewry....You have done more than anyone else to bring about the historic change in the attitude of the Church towards the Jewish people, initiated by the good Pope John XXIII, and to dress the gaping wounds that festered over many bitter centuries."[2]

What was it that Pope John Paul II did to advance the cause of Catholic-Jewish relations? Many deeds, words, and gestures stand out in the course of his long pontificate. Let me highlight a few key moments.

They say that the child is the father of the man, and John Paul II's affection for the Jewish people began in his home town of Wadowice, where as a child he had many Jewish friends and neighbors. Later he acutely felt their suffering during the Holocaust. It was only natural that the

Jewish people would have a special place in his heart when he became pope.

On April 13, 1986, John Paul II did something that no pope since Saint Peter had ever done: he visited a Jewish synagogue. The Italian newspaper *Il Giornale* captured the importance of this visit, noting that although the physical distance between the Vatican and the Synagogue of Rome was tiny, it had taken two thousand years for a pope to get there.

The visit to the synagogue of Rome gave the ultimate seal of approval to the new and warmer relationship between Christians and Jews. While there, John Paul II observed that Judaism is not external to Christianity, but is somehow inside it. What the pope seems to have meant is that we can only truly understand who we ourselves are as Catholics through coming to understand Judaism. Our own identity is somehow dependent upon the Jewish faith. When we begin to search the richness and depth of our own religion, we discover that we have a unique relationship with Judaism, of an altogether different quality from our relationship with any other non-Christian religion.

John Paul II (ably assisted by the then Cardinal Ratzinger) promoted the Vatican's recognition of the State of Israel (ambassadors were exchanged in 1994). This recognition was of huge significance, not only for the Jewish population in Israel, but also for the worldwide Jewish community. Many Christians have little or no idea how important the State of Israel is for Jewish identity. It is deeply rooted in the Jewish mind and heart, and has been for almost 4,000 years, since God promised Abraham to guide him into a special land. Although Jews were scattered around the world for centuries, they never really left this land. Each Passover they prayed, "Next year in Jerusalem." At each wedding, they smashed a glass to remind them they were a broken people, cut off from their true home. Zionism, the desire to return to the Jewish homeland, was first articulated over 2,500 years ago during the exile in Babylon. But it was not until the nineteenth century that Zionism took on a political form.

For the Jewish people, to renege on the land of Israel is tantamount to reneging on Scripture and on what God himself has promised. Christians, on the other hand, generally find it difficult to accept God's promise of this land to the Jewish people. We are afraid that if we recognize the biblical basis of the Jewish claim to the land of Israel, we will also be forced to go along with everything Israelis do there, such as allowing Jewish settlers to build on Palestinian territory. But it is possible to support the Jewish right to their homeland without supporting every Israeli policy that is implemented there—for the Bible that evokes the deep Jewish bond with the land also commands a profound responsibility toward the widow, the orphan, and the stranger. Despite the importance of the land, only human beings are created in God's image and likeness. Only people are sacred.

It is tragic that two groups of sacred people—Israelis and Palestinians—continue to suffer in this land. The State of Israel has the right to exist, and the Palestinian people have the right to live in dignity and freedom. There are no winners while violence continues. At the end of his trip to the Holy Land in May 2009, Pope Benedict XVI remarked that the wall separating one people from another was the saddest thing he had seen on his trip. We Christians are not called to choose Jews at the expense of Palestinians, or Palestinians at the expense of Jews. We are called to love everyone equally. We are also called to hope. The Northern Irish poet Seamus Heaney, himself no stranger to divided communities, evokes the miracle of unexpected and welcome change in *The Cure at Troy*, his adaptation of a play by

Sophocles. Although history teaches us not to hope, there sometimes arises the most wonderful of transformations, when, as Heaney puts it, "hope and history rhyme." There are even more powerful images in the Bible itself of a messianic age when the wolf will live peacefully with the lamb (Isa 11:6), and when no one will be hurt on the holy mountain of God (Isa 65:25). The mere fact of this messianic vision is already an invitation to move beyond division and antagonism. But for the moment, this vision of peace in diversity seems far away for many who live in Israel and the occupied territories.

One of the most moving gestures of Pope John Paul II's entire pontificate was his insertion of a written prayer into a crack of the Western Wall of the Temple during his visit to Jerusalem in March 2000. The Western Wall has a special sacredness for the Jewish psyche: it has been a place of veneration, prayer, and pilgrimage for centuries. There was something profoundly touching about Pope John Paul II, carrying the weight of the years, making his way slowly and haltingly toward this Wall, bowing his head in silence and praying, and inserting his written prayer into a small crevice.

This written prayer expressed deep sadness for those who throughout history caused Jewish suffering. It pleaded for God's forgiveness and pledged itself to an authentic brotherhood with the Jewish people. John Paul II's extraordinary gesture blazed a trail for millions of Christians around the world. We are invited to take up his invitation, to reach out to Jews with humility and honesty. Through this encounter, we will learn how to be better Christians.

Christianity is a unique faith with its own unique message. But it is not completely independent from Judaism. Its origins, development, and future are all intertwined with Judaism. Saint Paul has a vivid image that conveys this wonderfully. In the Letter to the Romans, chapter 11, Paul clearly says that Judaism is the root of the olive tree. The root gives life and nourishment. The new faith of Christianity is grafted as a branch onto the olive tree. If the branch cuts itself off from its root, it will die. For many centuries, Christians have tried to do precisely this, and have badly damaged the root, and also themselves, in the process. But the story is not totally negative: Christianity has also become a dynamic and life-giving branch, and has spread the savor and sap of Judaism to a wider world. Christians cannot be Christians without the Jewish people, but it is worth asking whether the reverse is also true. Strange and even offensive as it may seem to many Jews against the background of their long and tortured relationship with Christianity, the following question must be asked: can the Jewish people be Jews without Christians?

Whatever about the answer to this question, we have at least entered a new and better stage of history with one another. While not denying what divides us, we welcome the fact that we are no longer enemies but friends, that we are now companions instead of competitors. If good things still managed to happen despite our centuries-long antagonism, great things will occur now that we are beginning to become friends.

CHAPTER TWO

The Power of the Family

I don't know if we'll make it out. I want to tell you
that I love you and I love the kids.
                    Captain Walter Hynes, New York Fire
                    Department, September 11, 2001

What if you knew you were about to die? Not in six months or
three weeks, but in a matter of minutes? How would you cope?

When the victims of 9/11 were faced with only minutes
to live, they could have denied the obvious. They could have
pretended to themselves that this nightmare was not happening. Or they could have given up completely and sunk
into helpless hopelessness. But, in fact, the information we
have suggests that many of them did something totally different. They held their world as close as they could one last
time. They became as alive as they had ever been. They did
not spew out words of bitterness, nor did they lash out at
anyone. In those fateful moments, they pared away all the
extraneous stuff and got to the essential. They did something
simple yet marvelously profound: they phoned and left messages for their families to say how much they loved them. It
would have been understandable if they had become frozen
by fright, utterly overwhelmed by their tragic fate. Instead,
again and again, they thought of significant others in their
lives, giving voice to their love and devotion. "Please tell my

children that I love them very much," said United Airlines flight attendant CeeCee Lyles in a message to her husband. "I love you, honey," said Tom Burnett, a passenger on Flight 93, to his wife Deena. At the very moment their own lives were about to be extinguished, these firefighters, workers, and citizens thought above all of others.

These victims testified to the undying strength of the familial bond. They knew they loved and were loved, and so they could meet death. When we follow the law of love in our families, we can face any kind of trial or sacrifice. The family is an institution of capital importance for our personal and social lives. With a good family behind us, we can conquer the world, for although the family is the smallest institution in the world, it is also the greatest. It is much smaller than a state, a county, a town, or a village. But it is also greater, because it predates all of them. Before vast empires ever arose, tiny families had already been thriving for an age. Before even villages existed, families were there. Without the family, there would never have been villages, towns, cities, or nations in the first place. The family is one of the most marvelous gifts of God. It is the institution that shapes human character like no other. Families blossom when there is love, mutual respect, and obedience. But when hatred reigns, when Cain kills his brother Abel, the family becomes a nightmare scenario, and unleashes destruction and suffering like nothing else:

> For sweetest things turn sourest by their deeds;
> Lilies that fester smell far worse than weeds.
>
> (Shakespeare, Sonnet 94)

For better or worse, for richer or poorer, in sickness or in health, each of us carries our family inside us—for all the days of our lives. We do not merely carry our family as a memory, but as a determining influence on the way we act and behave. Our very bodies are shaped by our parents. We talk and look like them. We unconsciously imitate their gestures and walk with a similar gait. One day I told off a friend who was exasperating me, and she laughed, saying, "They're exactly the words your father uses!" Our psyches bear our parents' influence in an even deeper way. We inherit so many values, spoken and unspoken, from our families. The goals we pursue owe much to our family's ambitions—and to our reaction against their aspirations. The family is a web from which we can never disentangle ourselves, and from which we never truly want to become unstuck.

The 9/11 story shows that we still instinctively see the family as central to our lives. Yet today there is disagreement about whether the family should continue to play a central role in society. Even though the family structure persists, in some cases it is barely recognizable from what it was a generation ago. We find new relational configurations of same-sex couples who procure children with the help of surrogate mothers or sperm-donor fathers. Despite pushing key moral boundaries, these alternative "families" are modeled in so many ways on the traditional family that they paradoxically witness to our longing for the traditional familial setup.

In the West, there is tolerance for unusual and avant-garde relational configurations, but the traditional family is no longer in vogue. Even the phrase "family values" has become a bad expression in the minds of many progressively minded people. For them it symbolizes blind and unthinking adherence to narrow-minded and out-of-date morality. In this context the question arises: is it possible to live as Christian families in today's world?

The task is certainly more difficult and challenging than ever before. Formerly, Western societies identified to some extent with Christian values. Because many Christians lived in an environment that supported the family unit, their commitment could survive without being deeply rooted. Now the West has become increasingly de-Christianized. Because the cultural climate around us is so unsettled, our roots must go deeper into the soil of our faith if we are to weather the storm.

The first two ingredients for a Christian family are a man and a woman who pledge to make something fundamentally unified out of themselves without compromising their two unique and distinctive personalities. The Book of Genesis tells us that a man leaves his father and mother and joins himself to his wife, and the two become one flesh. We also know from the Book of Genesis that this astonishing unity did not last long: once Adam and Eve rebelled against God, they also ruptured the harmony between themselves.

For many people, the idea of two becoming one for a lifetime is totally unrealistic, a pure pipe dream. Even when Jesus spoke of marriage being forever, his own disciples found it practically impossible to accept—they felt it would be more advisable not to marry at all (see Matt 19:10). I was so emotionally immature in my twenties and thirties that if I had married a woman then instead of taking the road to priesthood, she may very well have filed for a quick divorce. It needed God's unconditional love to put up with me! Marriages fail, as do priests in their vocations. A priest cannot remain a priest (or at most can only be a pale imitation of the true thing) if he does not cultivate his relationship with God. A husband and wife who are humanly mature can ensure a successful union by inviting God into their lives as well as each other.

If a husband and wife do not bring God into their lives, something or someone else will imagine their lives for them, whether it is their favorite pop song or *Cosmopolitan* magazine. Even with God in their lives, there is no magic formula to attain instant relational success, but there is the marvel of a deep and steady transformation of each partner that enables both of them to live and act as they truly are—images of God. We are called to love one another as God loves us, gratuitously and with no strings attached. Being loved in return is a great gift, but a husband and wife are not to love each other merely in order to seek that reward. They are not to love each other only when they feel like loving. Their love is certainly helped by feelings, but it based on something much more solid and lasting: a solemn promise and commitment they made to each other. Scripture is full of practical guidelines that married couples can put into practice. The Gospel of Matthew tells us that if we are about to offer our gift at the altar, and remember that a brother or sister has something against us, we should leave immediately and be reconciled. Then we can return and offer our gift. The Letter to the Ephesians commands us not to let the sun go down on our anger. Instead of allowing resentments to fester, we should settle our differences as quickly as possible. Scripture constantly invites us to speak the truth from our heart, with kindness and compassion.

What about the relationship between parents and children? Let me start with how parents can learn from their children. Children are the greatest teachers of all, so much so that Jesus tells us not simply to pay attention to them, but to become like them ourselves. Jesus is not canonizing childhood, but he is telling us that there is a great treasure in the spirit of childhood. There is something wonderful about the adult who remains faithful to the child that he or she once was. Childhood is the true heart of everything. The strange thing is that, once you have lost childhood, you can only get it back by becoming a saint.

The most important commandment Christians must exercise in relation to the family is to honor our fathers and mothers. It is all too easy to take parents for granted, and forget how much we are indebted to them. That's why God commands us to honor them in a special way. They give us the gift of life, wash us, clothe us, work to put bread on our table, get up in the middle of the night to calm our fears, and put themselves out to provide for our every need, often making big sacrifices in the process. They are our first teachers in life and in virtue, and hopefully our best. They are the first ambassadors of God that are sent our way. They are our first friends, and much better friends than some of those to whom we later open our hearts. When we fail to honor our parents, we fail to honor those who are next to God in importance. When we betray our parents' love, we are on the road to betraying all future loves. A good-for-nothing son or daughter will become a bad husband or wife. A cruel son or daughter will become a wicked adult.

However, respect is not a one-way affair in the family. Parents are also obliged to love and respect their children. Nature gives them a head start, so that for most parents this love is instinctive. They can add to this instinctive love by giving a good example, teaching their children to be honest, decent, and upright, to be disciplined, and to respect the rights of others. Parents can encourage their children with kind words, and lift words of praise together with them to God. They should have high hopes for their children, but not unreasonable expectations. A boy always sees in his mother the image of the bride he wants to marry, and a daughter sees in her father the husband for whom she longs. If a mother and a father lead good lives, they will give their children invaluable help when it comes to choosing whom to marry. Parents who display little or no interest in the material and spiritual well-being of their own children do them a profound disservice. If much of the evil we see in individuals can be traced back to bad friendships, much of it can ultimately be traced back to the bad friendship of those who were meant to be their first and best friends.

Despite the risks it entails, God has repeatedly chosen the family to reach the heart of all of humanity. God made a covenant with Abraham, promising a son to him and his barren wife Sarah. The covenant was realized when Sarah, defying all human expectations, gave birth to Isaac. Later, God made a covenant with a virgin called Mary, and, under Joseph's care, she gave birth to Jesus and to a new world.

Each family is an intimate web of relationships that reaches back in time, into the remote past. I've only been able to trace my ancestry back to John Casey, who was born in Mayo in 1841. I'm proud of that man. He was only four years old when the Great Famine hit Ireland with a vengeance, as a result of a potato blight. I have no idea how he survived, especially because he grew up in the poorest part of Ireland at the time, County Mayo. One in four Irish people died or emigrated between 1845 and 1852: Ireland still has a much smaller population today than it did in 1841. But it is thanks to John that I am here. Something of him is still alive in my genes. The family sinks its roots into an unknown past, and looks forward to the future through children and grandchildren. I look into the eyes of my nieces and nephews, and I see a new and exciting world taking shape.

Ideally, the family is a space in which children are reared, find security, and learn how to trust and love; a place where children care for parents as well, in a mutual and lifelong framework of love and responsibility. Fundamentally, the family is about giving and receiving life.

Traditionally in Western culture (and still today in many other cultures), the crucial elements making up a family were marriage between a man and woman, and a household with children. There is no doubt that many married relationships were far from ideal, and there were shortcomings in the traditional framework: women had no guarantee of being treated equally, the father wielded excessive power, and many children were forced to work from a young age, missing out on childhood. But whatever the drawbacks of the traditional family structure, it helped countless generations. Society was geared toward supporting the family. Society expected marriage to work; it wanted couples to remain together and have children; it frowned on divorce, considering it a last-ditch solution to be used only in the most extreme of cases.

In Western societies and in certain others, the traditional pattern has largely broken down. There is no longer an expectation of monogamy, lifelong commitment, and children. When the going gets tough, divorce is seen by many as a reasonable option. What future is there for the family? Will it recover its previous position as a prime foundational unit of Western culture or continue to morph into multiple forms? Will marriage provide a stable structure to embark on life's journey or only a temporary halting site? What happens to the fabric of society when individuals make a lasting promise of marriage, only to break it readily if things do not work out as they anticipate?

Should children be reduced to pawns in acrimonious struggles between divorced parents? Should their lives be split in two because their parents break up? What happens to the relationship with the parent who adopts the role of visiting parent, having regular or only intermittent access to the children? How can children be helped to deal with the feelings of being alone and unwanted that can overcome them when their parents divorce, and when the unresolved anger about their parents' conduct stays with them long afterward? What if only one parent wants to divorce? Should that parent's preference decide things? What if the other parent and the children want to save the marriage? Whose wants and needs are more important? If one or both partners try to make it work as best they can but fail, should they continue to live together? What can be done to support single parents—the vast majority of whom are mothers—as they try to raise children on their own?

In the case of sperm donors and surrogate mothers, who is the real mother or father? Is the identity of the egg or sperm donor really irrelevant? Is it fair for children that the genetic mother or father remains anonymous? Have adopted and test-tube children the right to know at least the genetic history of their biological parents so they can anticipate future health problems? What does it do to a child to discover that its father or mother will be forever untraceable? Or to learn that it is a designer baby, paid for in the belief that it would turn out to be a special kind of child? And if it does not turn out to be the genetic wonder its parents hoped for, how will this affect the child—and the parents?

What effect is the shortage of women having in the two most populated nations in the world—China and India? What about the unborn children whose lives were cut short all too soon, before they could become a visible part of their families? Were there, among them, the twenty-first-century equivalents of Abraham Lincoln, Helen Keller, Mahatma Gandhi, Martin Luther King, or Mother Teresa? Have we missed out on inspirational figures that could have touched our lives and changed our world for the better? Are we the poorer for the fact that they never saw the light of day? Ronald Reagan once observed that everyone in favor of abortion is already born.

The family has a decisive influence on our personalities and destinies. We are always born within some human context. We enter the world from the body of a woman. She may be single, married, or divorced. She may have a loving and supportive partner or a violent and abusive one. The family environment may be poor, comfortable or affluent; parents may be literate or illiterate, emotionally mature or immature. All these factors affect our prospects in life. We do not begin from the same starting point. It would be great if we were all equal, but the way the cards are dealt, some are more equal than others.

Our characters and personalities develop over the course of life. The process begins in the family, whatever form the family may take. It is there that children first learn to love or to hate, to be kind or to be manipulative, to serve or to dominate. The family is the fundamental school for life. If children only learn injustice in the family, it will be extraordinarily difficult for them to construct a just culture as adults. If they are taught how to lie and deceive, it will be a big challenge for them to help build a transparent society later on.

Despite all the controversy about the role of the family in Western culture, there is something profoundly reassuring about the fact that many people still believe in its value. The Universal Declaration of Human Rights promulgated by the United Nations in 1948 declared that the family is the fundamental unit of society. This is not a statement about how things are, but about how things ought to be. It is not a description of the state of the family, but a formulation of an ideal for the family. It is not an empirical fact, but a value. Even when the state of the family does not correspond to this value, we still want the family to reach the heights of this value: we want the family to be the core of society.

This value is deeply reassuring because through it we are saying that we do not want either the individual or individualism to constitute the fundamental reality in society. At the base and foundation of each society, we want there to be a group of individuals called family who are connected by deep and lasting bonds. At the heart of culture, we want an altruistic structure instead of a constant bias toward self-interest. A man and a woman voluntarily come together, ready to give of themselves for the long-term and to make sacrifices in order to bring children into the world and rear them. As long as the institution of the family endures, whatever the shortcomings and failures of particular families, we will have an institution that is bigger than one person, a structure that of its nature tends to surpass the narrow confines of selfishness and egoism. The family is a sign of hope that self-preservation is not the first and last word in our world.

I cannot finish this chapter without saying something about fatherhood. In a way, I am not up to this challenge: although many people call me "Father," I am aware that my title does not stand up to close scrutiny; after all, I am not a biological father. But I nevertheless would like to share my reflections, many of which are the fruit of father figures in my own life, and some of which I have gleaned from my own fatherly roles.

Over the last number of years, I have become the sad witness to many men's flight from fatherhood. I have seen priests leave the priesthood. I have seen men separate from their wives and lose their children, and in the process become deprived of their own fatherhood. Even in best-case scenarios, men can become so completely taken up by their work that they are reluctant to do much more than sign checks for their children. The disappearance of fathers is unnoticed by many, but it is one of the greatest crises facing world culture. Without a healthy relationship with fathers, infants and young children become radically insecure. Fathers give children courage: the readiness to take risks, the willingness to be intellectually curious, and the strength to become more and more independent. If we want a better future for our children, we must factor in fathers.

Mothers and motherhood enjoy a positive image in the public mind, and rightly so. But fathers and fatherhood have fallen on hard times. At the same time that fathers are under the spotlight, there are also new demands being made upon them, above all the expectation that they will take an active and involved role in their children's lives. Today's men are willing to get their hands dirty with changing the diapers or doing the housework, but parts of their new role leave them at a loss: how can they help their children develop emotionally? How can they help them be at ease with the masculine world? In the past, being a good father did not explicitly entail such demands, and so today's fathers have no role models to fall back on. The fathers of the past were expected to be financial providers, but were often not required to invest emotionally in their children. The requirement to be more than a mere breadwinner is daunting. It is new and unmapped territory. The fathers of today have little or no experience from their own past to teach them about the huge difference a supportive and nurturing father can make.

Women have the opportunity to prepare for motherhood through pregnancy. As they feel their own body change and grow over a period of nine months, they receive an acute visible reminder of what is about to happen, and once their baby is born, they are physically equipped to breastfeed them. Men do not have a visible role already planned out so plainly. Once a man has made love and his wife has become pregnant, his physical role in the emergence of the new child seems over. To be an expectant father means to accept what is happening in a passive way, to watch everything from a distance, and this distance can make him feel uninvolved and even alienated. How many expectant fathers are invited to ante-natal classes? How many are ever even briefed by their wife's gynecologist? How many receive paternity leave? It is all too easy for fathers to receive the subliminal message that they are only second-class parents while the center stage belongs to mothers.

But none of this means that fathers are expected to be merely warm, fuzzy, chummy beings for their children. The father helps his young children best by enabling them to let go of their mother, by showing them that there are brave and breathtaking ways to live beyond the intimate attachment to their maternal anchor. Of course he should help them make this transition using gentleness and grace. He also helps the mother let go of her children by reassuring and supporting her at this moment of separation.

There is a double-edged temptation for any father: either to make fatherhood such an absolute that he becomes completely authoritarian or to dissolve fatherhood so much that his relationship with his children becomes bland and insipid, without any link of authority. In Western society, the more robust side of fatherhood has a bad name, and words like *paternal* and *patriarchal* have a negative connotation. This bad name is not without reason. If children have never had a relationship with their father or had one where they were excessively punished or abused (Eph 6:4 warns: "Fathers, do not provoke your children to anger"), they are likely to develop a strong distaste for any kind of father figures, whether teachers or tutors, police or politicians.

The traditional image of fatherhood was often too narrow and restrictive. But is the solution to be an uncertain father, or a distant or peripheral one? There is a balance between these two unhelpful poles: it is the model of fatherhood based on authority instead of authoritarianism, on service instead of servility, on leadership without pride, and on discipline without repression.

The right balance is hard to find. A sensitive mother can help a father walk the healthy line between extremes: her natural compassion will intervene to stop a father becoming too severe, but she will also not hesitate in invoking the father as an authority figure for the child.

The pop culture young people imbibe does not reflect a balanced picture of fatherhood but often only one of the polarities: complete severity or no authority at all. For instance, a lot of pop music has sometimes rightly, but more often wrongly, slammed father figures, and sometimes because of the musicians' own experience: The punk movement of the 1970s is most famously or notoriously represented by the Sex Pistols, whose bass player, Sid Vicious, had an absent father and heroin-addicted mother, and lived on the streets as a child. Grunge music of the early 1990s is typified especially by Nirvana; its lead singer, Kurt Cobain—who later took his own life—confessed that most of the anguish in his music was triggered by his parents' divorce. In the early 2000s, rap music can be typified by the best-selling and highly aggressive white rapper Eminem, who was brought up by his mother after his father abandoned them when he was barely two years of age.

But one of my favorite pop songs gives a redeeming image of fatherhood, though it is forced to turn to the Ultimate Father to find someone who truly cares. It is the 2003 antiwar anthem "Where is the Love?" by the Los Angeles hip-hop group the Black-Eyed Peas. The chorus is a prayer:

> Father, Father, help us. Send some guidance
>   from above
> 'Cause people got me, got me questioning' where is
>   the love?[1]

To have a father is to sense that you are not the one who started your own life. You are not at the beginning of everything. You are linked with someone who came before you. In the etymological sense of the word, to have a father is to be "religious." The Latin verb *religare* has the connotation "to tie, to bind." You have a bond, a tie. You are linked to someone who precedes you, related to someone beyond and before yourself.

Everyone needs a father. Having a father gives you a firmer sense of who you are, of where you come from. Without a father, you feel weak and fragile, and you are never certain. You feel disinherited and denied, dispossessed and deprived.

Of course, it is important what kind of father you have. Children do not want a father who denies them freedom, whose power usurps their liberty, who lives their life for them instead of allowing them to live their own. Children flourish with a father who says "Son,…all that is mine is yours" (Luke 15:31). You don't want a father who takes everything away from you, but instead one who encourages you, who gives generously.

Fathers are in short supply these days. The absence of fathers is not simply a problem in secular culture. Fathers are also missing in the religious world. While giving a sermon, an Irish priest-friend recently mentioned his regret at missing the experience of human fatherhood. I guess he was indirectly trying to affirm the importance of the role of the parents who sat before him. He was also being honest about a sadness he felt inside. Later in his sermon, he went on to paint a picture from his ministry that showed how much of a spiritual father he was to young people. I imagine it was hard for him to name his own fatherly identity for what it was.

But beyond the shortage of priests and the difficulty of naming our spiritual fatherhood, there is also the challenge of appropriating and owning the fact that we as priests are fathers. In secular culture, many fathers are retreating in fear from their identity and role as fathers; something similar is happening among priests. I am not thinking primarily of the obvious problem of fathers who leave mothers with the burden of bringing up children alone, or of absent fathers who no longer have any link with their children, or of priests who leave their priesthood. I am thinking especially of the many fathers who prefer to act as brothers with their kids, whereas what children really need is a father—and then similarly, of the priests who are in danger of losing their saltiness and becoming tasteless and insipid.

It is not easy being the father of a family—you have to rise in the middle of the night to reassure a crying child. You have to say to your kids, "You must be home by 11:00 p.m.," whereas they want to stay out past midnight. I learned something about how fathers of families must claim their authority when I lived and worked in a residence for college students. It was like being a father of sorts for an enormous family of young men on the threshold of adulthood. I was thoroughly annoyed the first time I had to get up at 3:00 a.m. in the morning to shush students. They were surprised that I was so angry. It did not make sense to them. I am sorry now that I displayed my anger that night. Certainly my feeling of anger clued me in to something important, but I should have controlled the emotion and channeled it in a productive way. They did not expect a father figure to be angry because his sleep was interrupted, although they could certainly understand my concern that the sleep of fellow students was being interrupted. In other words, the students expected me to be selfless: they felt I should be worried only if it was for their sake or the sake of others. Those students taught me something valuable. It took me time to find the right balance in my fatherly role there, to keep calm, and to deal with students kindly yet firmly.

Saint Joseph is a model of this fatherly selflessness. When he is asked out of the blue to get up in the middle of the night, he does not stop to think of his own comfort because he is focused on Mary and Jesus: "An angel of the Lord appeared to Joseph in a dream and said, 'Get up, take the child and his mother, and flee to Egypt'" (Matt 2:13).

I experienced two principal ways of being a father when I lived in that college dorm: first, through being present, being available—listening to students, talking with them, mentoring them, and praying with them; second, the nitty-gritty of challenging them to become adults and to act in a way that respected themselves and others. This regularly brought me into forceful dialogue with students, into straight-talking situations that demanded courage, tact, and a large expenditure of psychic energy. They almost always produced good fruit. Both of these methods of being a father are challenging—each in a different way. The ministry of presence requires us to set aside our own agenda in favor of being present to the people before us. The second method—clarifying boundaries, saying when enough is enough in a decisive but kind way—is a major challenge for fathers of any kind. Instead of speaking out, we can be tempted to keep silent and let things go. Indeed, fathers in families and priestly fathers are not sure how to exercise authority now that they feel they have little effective power. They are radically uncertain about their role.

Today, the authority of fathers must come above all from the persons they are. It has to radiate outward from their character. Especially vital is the relationship that exists between fathers and those they serve. If people trust a father figure and see the purity, integrity, and conviction of a man who lives what he teaches, they will accord him authority. It was this integrity and purity that had people spellbound when they listened to Jesus, "for he taught them as one having authority, and not as their scribes" (Matt 7:29).

The people we serve help us to uncover, articulate, and strengthen our own fatherhood. I have seen how the experience of becoming a father of a newborn baby brings out a whole new dimension in a man's nature. He gets in touch with a new compassion. He experiences a reaffirmation of himself as protector and provider, as nourisher and nurturer. Through becoming a father he also has the chance to become a better man. Not only is fatherhood a grace for the man himself, it is also a great gift for children, because along with the mother he has the privilege of teaching his children what it means to be human, and of being God's first ambassador to them.

Children are more than gratified when a father figure believes in them. But not every father believes in children. Ultimately, to be fathers worthy of the name, whether we are natural fathers or stepfathers, teachers or mentors, we need the help of the ultimate Father, who has an astonishing vision for each one of his children:

> For this reason I bow my knees before the Father, from whom every family in heaven and on earth takes its name. I pray that, according to the riches of his glory, he may grant that you may be strengthened in your inner being with power through his Spirit, and that Christ may dwell in your hearts through faith, as you are being rooted and grounded in love. I pray that you may have the power to comprehend, with all the saints, what is the breadth and length and height and depth, and to know the love of Christ that surpasses knowledge, so that you may be filled with all the fullness of God. (Eph 3:14–19)

CHAPTER THREE

Teachers Will Shine as Bright as Stars

You can get all A's and still flunk life.
                                    Walker Percy

As part of my training for the priesthood, I was asked to spend two years teaching in a high school. Actually, I was ordered rather than asked, because teaching was the last thing I wanted to do. I was twenty-four years of age and scared to death of standing in front of a class of thirty pupils only a few years younger than myself. I remember pleading to be sent as a missionary to the jungles of South America instead—where I would have probably lasted a week or so before succumbing to some tropical illness. That's how desperate I was. But my superiors were adamant: teaching German, French, and religious studies to Dublin teenagers was God's will for me.

One of the reasons I had no interest in becoming a teacher was because I did not retain particularly fond memories of school myself, and happily concurred with George Bernard Shaw's quip that the only time his education had been broken off was during his years at school. I had attended a Christian Brothers' school. Apart from the school principal, there weren't many brothers among the teaching staff, but their largely authoritarian and narrow spirit pervaded the place. In my five years there, I had one particularly good teacher, and another who bordered on being great. The really good teacher was a layman in love with his subject—the French language. He did not always show great faith in our abilities, and at times he gave the impression that he found it more than trying to put up with us, but for the most part he built on the positive, and did not put us down with his sense of humor. He always welcomed questions. He was a purist when it came to teaching French, believing that the only way to learn the language well was to be immersed in it from day one, so he talked to us all the time in those beautiful, nasal tones that make French at once so appealing and so snobbish. This game plan worked for those who were swept up by his enthusiasm, but for those who did not catch the bug, he was unwilling to compromise with a more pragmatic approach.

The teacher who was borderline great was a young Christian Brother who had just arrived at the school, full of life and enthusiasm. The first time he entered our classroom to teach religious studies he definitely broke the mold. He turned on the stereo and played a tune by Simon and Garfunkel. We couldn't believe it. No one had ever done this before. We hadn't even known that a brother was human enough to be interested in pop music. He did not just believe in the power of pop music; he also believed in our potential, which was a completely new experience. He listened to us and took what we said seriously. As well as liking his subject, he liked us, too.

Most of the other teachers varied from poor to fair to adequate. Some teachers had the potential to be better than they were, but the ethos of the school did not encourage them to nurture big expectations with regard to students. The teachers had an important but narrow focus: to ensure we did well in our exams. They had no larger aspirations for us. They obviously presumed we would make no great difference in the world, no creative contribution to society. Their view was not as impoverished as that of the character Thomas Gradgrind, who makes the following proclamation at the start of Charles Dickens' novel *Hard Times*: "Now, what I want is, Facts. Teach these boys and girls nothing but Facts. Facts alone are wanted in life. Plant nothing else, and root out everything else."[1] But their view was not a huge improvement on Gradgrind's either. They saw their task as filling our minds with necessary information rather than opening us to wisdom, ensuring rote memorization instead of character formation.

A few teachers were extremely volatile, prone to explode into violent rages, and were prepared to lash out when some poor unfortunate did not come up with the correct answer or went overboard in playing the class clown. A couple of times when I was a smart-mouth, I was sent to the principal's office, and received the mandatory lashes on the palm of my hand. The principal always had a purpose-made leather strap on his person. This brother was fair but strict, and no one wanted to cross him. Education with the Christian Brothers was largely a one-way street. We were the blank slates and they gave us the facts that we were meant to memorize and regurgitate. It wasn't that creativity was frowned upon; it simply never entered the picture. As a rule, they did not feel we had anything really worthwhile to offer, and so neither did we. All they expected were the correct answers. Otherwise, we were to keep our mouths shut. Any hint of unorthodox behavior was quickly suppressed. Too much self-expression on our part would bring them outside their comfort zone and force them to think outside the box, and they felt unequal to that challenge.

So a number of years later, when I arrived as a rookie teacher at a top Jesuit high school, I was full of ambivalence. I did not like teachers, and now here I was, one of them, fraternizing with the enemy. I had suffered from authoritarian and petty-minded discipline, and I resolved not to impose the same suffering on anyone else. Plus, I was by nature a disorganized person. No one gave me a training course, because they automatically presumed I was ready for the task. The only advice I received was, "Don't smile before Christmas." All of this proved to be a recipe for chaos. Christmas arrived on the second day of class: I smiled, and that was it. A bad Christmas it turned out to be! My classes were soon out of control. It was the Wild West. The students enjoyed being the outlaws, while I felt completely unable to play the role of lawman. Where do you begin when pandemonium reigns? Whom do you tell first to sit down? When there are so many kids running about, throwing things at each other, and making noise, they cannot even hear you yell anyway. Descartes said, "I think, therefore I am." I felt, "I'm inaudible and invisible, therefore I'm not." Even when my classes were not chaotic, there was always a constant undercurrent of noise, like the annoying buzz on a badly tuned FM channel. I was just relieved to make it to the end of each day without succumbing to a nervous breakdown.

Fast-forward to today, and I am fortunate to be teaching at the most prestigious pontifical university in Rome, and in the world. That is because I have been lucky enough to learn a few important lessons in the years in between. Above all, I've had the opportunity to reflect on my experience—the greatest school of all—and learn from it. One exercise I found particularly helpful was to sit down again and again with my Bible in hand, and read the account of the call of the prophet Jeremiah, comparing it to my own uncertain call to become a teacher. God had set Jeremiah apart before his birth and already appointed him a prophet at that early stage. This spurred me to reflect upon what had led me to be a teacher, and I began to see that in the midst of all my feelings of inadequacy and moments of resistance, God was steadily leading me (admittedly in a circuitous way that I did not recognize at the time) toward an incredibly valuable and worthwhile profession. At the same time, I completely identified with Jeremiah's initial resistance to his vocation as a prophet. Jeremiah turns to God and says, "Truly I do not know how to speak, for I am only a boy" (Jer 1:6). As a rookie teacher I lacked confidence in so many ways. I felt too young and wet behind the ears. I felt that none of my students wanted to listen to me. I felt I had nothing to offer. God responds robustly to Jeremiah's fear. "Do not say, 'I am only a boy,'" God replies. "You shall go to all to whom I send you, and you shall speak whatever I command you. Do not be afraid of them, for I am with you to deliver you" (Jer 1:7–8).

It was when I went on my first school trip that everything changed. I picked up a guitar and started to sing. The students found this totally cool. They were amazed: this new teacher who was struggling to control classes could actually rock big time! By singing a few songs, I somehow created a deep personal connection with those who listened. At that moment I felt rescued. God was saying to me, "I am with you."

Now I see that God too is a teacher. God formed me through my family and upbringing. God chose me to be born in Ireland in my particular family at this time in world history, with all the people and events that have shaped me. He chose me to be born the day I was born, and not a day earlier or later, at the hour I was born, and not another hour, to leave my mother's womb at the very moment I did. Even before I was born, God formed me and knitted me together inside her. Today God continues to shape me: God is my best educator. As the Book of Genesis tells us, God creates out of chaos. I am glad that God can deal with chaos so easily, because I set more than enough chaos before him. At an individual level, there is the bedlam of being busy and running after so many things, too many of which do not matter in the long run; the turmoil of strong feelings of elation or despair that can so easily overcome me; the unruliness of so many bright ideas filling my mind that my head can overheat in the process. At the interpersonal level, there is the confusion of finding a relationship entering difficult waters without advance warning. At a social level, there is the economic disarray and political madness that make life around me and my own at times so fragile and precarious.

For all these reasons and more, I am drawn to the mesmerizing images of God the Teacher in the song of Moses in chapter 32 of the Book of Deuteronomy. These images tell how God found his people in a howling desert wasteland, and surrounded them all with loving care, shielding and guarding them as the apple of his eye. Like an eagle, God spread wide wings to gather them and raised them up. The mantle of God's compassion transformed the harsh desert journey into peaceful progress toward a better future. Each time I have called on God in my own life, the Divine One has turned the parched land into springs of water; the Lord has carried me on eagles' wings.

When I was a rookie teacher, it never struck me that God too was a teacher, nor did it enter my head how important teaching was. Now I see that teaching is one of the noblest (and most demanding) professions in the world. Teaching that is carried out with a good heart is an immense act of love, because the instruction of those who are on the threshold of knowledge transforms lives and opens up new worlds. As well as pedagogical gifts, a teacher requires extraordinary delicacy and tact: things you say to a student at that impressionable age will never be forgotten. The actions and deeds of a teacher will always be remembered by students, either with gratitude or regret. Great teachers do not only teach their subjects; they also teach children that they are worthwhile. They do not only impart knowledge; they also give their hearts. Students imbibe life's lessons above all from the character of teachers. In the Book of Daniel, chapter 12, we read that those who are wise will shine as bright as the heavens, and those who lead many to righteousness will shine like the stars forever. Great teachers may not earn high salaries, but they receive a great reward in terms of fulfillment, as they witness how their efforts transform the lives of their students. For teachers of this caliber, seeing their students do well in life really makes their day. Their stars will surely glow without end.

Jesus was a teacher. "You call me Teacher and Lord—and you are right, for that is what I am" (John 13:13). For all that, he wasn't spared all the hard work and toil involved in teaching. His students did not understand what he was trying to teach them. How often do we find him repeating the same lessons over and over again to his disciples? Even after three years at his side, they still had not grasped the message. He had to go back over everything in the last week of his earthly life, and even after the Resurrection, he had to set them straight on many things.

Jesus the teacher wants Christians to use their heads. It was only a few years ago I realized that Jesus commands us to love God with our minds. Somehow it had escaped my attention before, even though he spelled out this commandment as clearly and unambiguously as possible. Perhaps because the commandment is so obvious, it is also so easy to overlook, like the purloined letter in Edgar Allan Poe's short story of the same name, in which a government minister hides a stolen letter in the most obvious place possible in his apartment, so that the police fail to find it although they comb the place from top to bottom. Or maybe it was because I simply never expected to be commanded to love God with all my mind. Yet this particular commandment is not a minor or unimportant one. On the contrary, it has absolute priority, because it is the first and most important commandment of all, as we discover in the Gospel of Matthew. A lawyer asks Jesus, "'Teacher, which commandment in the law is the greatest?' He said to him, 'You shall love the Lord your God with all your heart, and with all your soul, and with all your mind'" (Matt 22:36–37).

I had heard this commandment so often, but I had never noticed the word *mind*. Jesus tells us we are to love God with our *intelligence*. Of course, he also emphasizes the heart and soul, for love is a multifaceted thing. Education should nourish not only the intellectual dimension of our being, but all the rest as well.

We do not always use our heads when it comes to learning, at least not in much more than a mechanical manner. In Rome, I find that many Catholic seminarians who take courses in philosophy fail to connect it to their own way of living. One of my brightest students made a wonderful link between the most obscure area of philosophy—metaphysics—and the sexism that is rife in Italian culture. She pointed out that by truly taking to heart the difference between *substance* (something that exists in its own right, in and of itself, such as a rose), and *accidents* (things that exist only in something else, such as the scent and color of a rose), leering Italian men could change their lives. How? By deciding never again to judge a woman on the basis of her accidents (her physical appearance, her weight, the color of her hair and eyes), and instead resolving to approach her on the basis of her substance (all that remains unchanged in her despite the changes in her physical appearance). If every man decided to make a truth like this his personal point of reference, life as we know it for men and women on planet earth would be transformed. Imagine that each time a man meets a woman, he sees beyond her physical appearance in order to encounter the real person, the "substance." In this way, he applies the metaphysical distinction between substance and accidents to the way he lives his life. He acts in harmony with this newfound knowledge, and the relations between men and women are revolutionized as a result.

How do you help someone use their head? The English word *education* comes from the Latin verb *educere*, "to lead out." Socrates and Plato teach that learning is a kind of remembering of what we already have inside. It is a drawing out of our interior riches. There is a stirring scene that spells this out in the endearing French film *Être et Avoir*. Set in rural France, this 2002 documentary follows a school year in the life of thirteen pupils between the ages of four and eleven. They attend a tiny village school, where all are taught by one teacher in a single classroom. As the master Lopez is in the midst of teaching at the large table shared by the younger children, a four-year-old boy called Jojo asks, "Is it morning or afternoon?" If a four-year-old were to ask me that kind of question, my inclination would be to provide the correct answer immediately. But this superb teacher does things differently. He refuses the temptation to spoon-feed this young child. Instead, he turns to the other children around Jojo, and transforms Jojo's question into a splendid educational moment for everyone, remarking, "So, he is asking me if it's morning or afternoon." Now he has everyone in the loop. Then Lopez turns back to Jojo and asks, "Before the afternoon arrives, what do you do? You...." The boy responds, "Eat." Lopez then asks, "Have you eaten already?" Jojo says, "No." Lopez continues, "So it's still...." The little girl sitting next to Jojo answers, "Morning."[2] What a magnificent example of teaching a young child to use its head.

This is not an era for dumb disciples or witless Christians. Human beings are crying out for intelligence and wisdom. Certainly our world is thirsting for Christians who reach out to the poor and share their material possessions in lives of love. But our world is also hungering for Christians who lovingly share their intellectual gifts and treasuries of wisdom. Western culture is living out of ideas that have gone past their sell-by date; it is suffering from intellectual malnutrition. To regain its intellectual soundness, it needs to supplement its diet with intelligent Christianity. It is not a matter of concocting a menu of subtle, complex, and obscure ideas. It is a matter of presenting our culture with straightforward and true ones. These are the kind of ideas that can change the world.

In the Book of Genesis, God says to Abraham, "If I find at Sodom fifty righteous in the city, I will forgive the whole place for their sake" (Gen 18:26). Abraham bargains and negotiates with God, pleading greater leniency so that eventually God promises to save the entire city if there are ten innocent people to be found in it. In an analogous way, a whole culture can be saved from deterioration and decline if it possesses a handful of truly educated people—who have fully developed intellectually and humanly and act out of this fullness. Their hope and idealism are contagious. They plant seeds in others and help them water the roots of new knowledge.

Human intelligence penetrates reality, a fact already indicated by the derivation of the word *intellect* from the two Latin words *intus* and *legere*, together meaning "to read within." With our intelligence we seek to know the truth about things. We do so by removing the veil of strangeness and incomprehension between us and the world around us. We thus enter into a living and vital relationship with reality.

Wisdom takes intelligence a step further, for wisdom is not book knowledge, but practical knowledge. It applies knowledge to our lives. It translates our knowledge of the truth into ethical choices and moral decisions. Wisdom is the art of living that integrates knowledge into the fabric of our decision making and behavior. Without this living and lived wisdom, we get nowhere, or at least nowhere worthwhile. In order to attain such wisdom, our lives need to be focused on the good. We need to desire what is good. Wisdom does not mean forcing knowledge to correspond with how we want the world to be, but allowing our knowledge to harmonize with how the world is, with its fundamental goodness. If I have an incorrect goal in life, one imposed by my egoism and such prejudices as making as much money as possible, or merely furthering my career, this will blind my mind to what is truly worth doing.

When Hamlet is contemplating the possibility of death, Shakespeare has him muse, "The readiness is all" (*Hamlet*, 5.ii). To be ready, we need to prepare ourselves, figure things out, wrestle with issues and problems. Readiness is something we can muster up through hard work and willpower. But readiness alone is not enough. In Shakespeare's *King Lear*, Edgar says, "Ripeness is all" (*Lear*, 5.ii). Ripeness is similar to readiness, but there is nevertheless a crucial difference: ripeness is not the fruit of effort alone; the time has to be right, and the necessary growth must be gone through first. The sun must do its slow work of bringing the fruit to that perfect moment when it falls effortlessly. We need the help of a spiritual sun, of a higher power that is beyond us yet watches over us with a warm and radiant glow. The fruit will only fall when it has become ripe.

Readiness is all about our active preparation, efforts, strategies, and five-year plans—and these are vital as part of our response in an age of upheaval. But ripeness is indispensable as well. Ripeness is about who we are and whom we can count upon; it is about our relationships. In sum, it is about the quality of our lives more than the excellence of our plans. Without wisdom to guide intelligence, it can easily take the wrong detours: readiness minus ripeness does not bear good fruit. We must give direction to intelligence, and channel resources in a way that builds up our societies instead of fragmenting them even more. If we implement excellent theories but never visit the depths of our own humanity, we will continue to stumble along in an unbalanced and unhealthy way. We need to think with all of ourselves.

There are two crucial questions: Are we ripe? Are we ready? Both elements are vital in our Christian lives. Neither aspect cancels out the other. Both are valid, though not equally so, since ripeness has priority. Ripeness refers to who we are, to our being, to grace, to the gift of God that comes through communion. Readiness refers to what we do, to our effort, to our wrestling with intellectual questions. Grace is primary, and without grace our best efforts will be fruitless. Communion with God provides unity to our intellectual powers, adding ripeness to our readiness, and giving our lives unsuspected fruit. It is not the caliber of our arguments that will attract people, but the quality of our lives.

CHAPTER FOUR

Equality for Women

No one sex can govern alone. I believe that one of
the reasons why civilization has failed so lamenta-
bly is that it has had one-sided government.

Nancy Astor

There is a long way to go and much work to be done before
women receive the equality they deserve. There is continued
discrimination against women in many countries. At the
time of my writing this (despite murmurings of change),
women in Saudi Arabia are still not allowed drive cars, and
they cannot even appear in public without a male relative by
their side. Three quarters of the one billion people around
the world living in poverty are women. Three out of every
four illiterate adults on our planet are women. Most of the
work in our world is done by women, but the income they
receive in return is peanuts compared to what men are paid.
All in all, women get a raw deal. The American musician
Robert Mueller, on a visit to Burma in the 1950s, asked why
women were walking ahead of men after centuries of walking behind them. His Burmese host replied that it was
because there were unexploded land mines everywhere
since the war.

Women, as full human beings, are entitled to equal
rights. Some would suggest they are entitled to even more:

the psychologist Timothy Leary claimed that women who only seek equality with men are lacking in ambition. Many countries have enacted legislation to ensure the equality of women. But in practice, women still suffer unequal status in many countries, especially in political and social life, in the world of work, and in the family. Men become uneasy if women's intelligence and character prove as striking as their physical beauty. However, if noble principles cannot convince men to treat women better, enlightened self-interest should. We are facing such big challenges in our world today that we need the input and contribution of everyone, and not just men, in order to grapple successfully with the problems we face.

In 1963, Martin Luther King gave his historic "I have a dream" speech, in which he painted a future in which blacks and whites would live together in harmony as equals. Women want to be treated equally, nothing more and nothing less. We may dare dream of a future in which women will be treated as the equals of men, and we should do what we can to make this dream a reality. When that future arrives, feminism will come to an end, because it will have outlived its usefulness. Happily, it will be superfluous, having fulfilled its purpose. When that tomorrow comes upon us, we will inhabit a better world because it will do justice to both genders; and by freeing women, it will also unchain men.

There is legislation guaranteeing women's rights in Western culture. But there is some distance to go before women are treated equally. Until women play a central role in making new laws, there will still be an appreciable way to go. Discrimination against women remains in many areas. In education, many girls are told that they have no talent for math or science, and so are not granted the opportunity to develop the kinds of skills that are in high demand on today's labor market. Although technological developments have eased the working burden of wives and mothers, women are still weighed down with the majority of domestic chores such as cooking, shopping for groceries, and ferrying children to school and back. Men are steadily taking a greater share in household responsibilities, but women still bear the brunt of homemaking duties.

The burden on women is even heavier in the case of marital breakups, when children generally live with their mothers. Despite the extra pressure, a single mother with money and a steady income can usually cope with supporting children. But if she has to work long hours to make ends meet, this puts her under huge additional stress. It is not easy being both sole breadwinner and homemaker. As a rule, it is the woman who becomes economically poorer as a result of separation. She may receive child support, though the amount is often inadequate. And if she separates from a cohabiting partner, the father is not likely to pay child maintenance at all.

Working women still get paid less than male colleagues. If women were less qualified and had less to offer in the workplace, this discrepancy in pay would be understandable. But nowadays, working women are just as educated as men, and at times have a slight educational edge over their male coworkers. They have just as many degrees, they put in just as much hard work, they are handed just as many responsibilities, and they have just as many years of experience behind them—yet they are underpaid relative to male colleagues. The reason for the wage gap is simple: it is because they are women. Not only do women have to put up with sex discrimination; many still undergo sexual harassment in the workplace as well. Sexual harassment is as much about power as about sex: it is a way for men to control women and put them down.

When it comes to the public sphere, women are seriously underrepresented. In politics, the judiciary, government agencies, and leading positions in business, academia, and the media, there are substantially fewer women. These environments can prove particularly intimidating, and the fact that these milieus are so male-dominated makes it even harder for women to break into them. To make any inroads, they must challenge and change a well-established male ethos, and this is especially difficult when there are hardly any other women with a foothold inside these spheres to support them. Women's difficulties in public life are compounded by the often-intrusive media attention to which they are subject. Their private lives are scrutinized, their looks are discussed, their clothes are criticized. The media does this almost automatically, as it is already used to objectifying women in advertising and music videos.

Violence against women is widespread in the Western world. It happens among rich and poor, young and old. It is not limited to any socioeconomic class or age group. It takes many forms. Domestic violence is the most common. There is also physical assault, sexual assault, rape, prostitution, sadistic pornography, and the brutal treatment of women who are trafficked as sex slaves. Violence against women is probably underreported in the Western world because many women are convinced they will not obtain justice. One reason is because our culture can insidiously blame women themselves for the violence from which they suffer, suggesting that if they wore different clothes, behaved more demurely, stayed in at night, were less trusting of strangers, or separated from their partners at the first hint of trouble, they would not be attacked. In 1999, an Italian court sparked international outrage by ruling that women wearing tight jeans could not by definition be raped since the jeans were only capable of being removed with their collaboration and consent. It took almost a decade—until 2008—for this ruling to be reversed.

There are support mechanisms for women who suffer violence, though they are not always sufficient to help them pick up the pieces of their shattered lives. But at least there are various provisions to help them cope—crisis lines, counseling, women's shelters, restraining orders, legal advocacy, landmark legislation (for instance, the Violence against Women Act of 1994 in the United States), and sympathetic treatment from health care personnel, police, and the courts. All these support systems make a difference.

What can men do? Since men and women have lived cheek by jowl for millennia, it is difficult for men to stand back and see the inequality of women for what it really is. First, men need to recognize that they belong to a gender that for centuries has discriminated against women, both consciously and unconsciously. A major problem is that men often do not see there is a problem, and fail to recognize that they themselves play a big part in it. Overall, men are reluctant to ask if they operate out of a sexist worldview. Nonetheless, there are encouraging signs: more and more men are ready to change their attitudes. Since men have been primarily responsible for maintaining discrimination against women, discrimination can only be eliminated when men adjust the way they think and behave. But even when men work actively at changing themselves, they still cannot transform themselves without sustained effort. Even when they make genuine attempts to treat women as equals, they can find it extremely difficult to escape all their blind spots. If men's sense of self-esteem is built on unequal relationships with women, change is especially threatening, because it brings about a loss of self-worth. In such situations, it is tempting for men to retreat to a position of exercising power over women instead of choosing the difficult and vulnerable path of relating to women as equals.

In order to change in a real way, every man must recognize that he has conflicting desires when it comes to women: he wants to treat them equally, yet he also seeks to exercise power over them. Unless he admits this inner struggle between warring desires, he will deceive himself into imagining that it is only other men who are tempted to oppress women. He will fail to acknowledge his own complicity. No one is born full of generosity and compassion—we need to undergo conversion to become more human. When men change the way they think about women, they will also act in a different way toward them. Women are not asking for a huge shift in thought, simply the recognition that they are full human beings.

Some men make the mistake of thinking they have to reject everything that men stand for in order to be pro-women. They feel that the price of being on the side of women is to be against men and to feel perpetually guilty about their own manhood. They feel they must ignore their own needs and only respond to the needs of women. They feel obliged to be so in touch with their feminine side that they are convinced they must renounce masculinity. They become incredibly nurturing, but also spineless and weak-willed, retreating into a sheltered, motherly world and losing manly characteristics like the courage that rises to face risks and take on challenges.

But it is also true that men's idea of manhood is inadequate and needs deepening. For some men, manhood is all about control, and means being in charge of wife, children, and career. Their image of a true man is of a domineering type who bestrides the world like a giant Colossus. But real manhood is about a different kind of preeminence, not parading a larger ego than everyone else, but serving something truly significant: a cause worth living for. This does not necessarily entail becoming a Green Beret or an Arctic explorer. It may involve raising children to be persons of character, or it may mean volunteering to mentor troubled teenagers. Genuine manhood is not so much about being self-reliant as about being a self upon whom others can rely. Everyone can count on a true man: whatever he says, he does. He is as solid and consistent as rock. An authentic man is secure enough not to demand an incessant show of respect, and confident enough in himself that he can respect others without feeling threatened or undermined.

Even when individual men begin to take women seriously as human beings, they still do not know what it is to actually be a woman. They have not experienced womanhood from the inside, and they find it difficult to project themselves imaginatively into female concerns. But although they cannot stand in a woman's shoes, they do have a sense of what an equal society might look like. And it is this vision, however hazy, that animates their efforts to eliminate discrimination against women.

At the individual level, many men have already changed their mind-sets and their behavior. They have learned to refrain from physical or verbal acts of aggression, and to take an active part in housework and childcare. But collectively, men have been slow to take action to confront inequality. It is only through collective action that decisive change will occur, but collective action is not easily brought about. Men's groups are usually preoccupied with men's issues, and only indirectly or secondarily with women's concerns. It can be hard to convince men to engage collectively in a process that leads to a diminution of their own personal and social power. If men cannot see how taking a stance for women's equality can benefit them, they may have little desire to commit themselves to this way of acting. All they behold is a scenario where they forfeit privilege. It is much more energizing for women to be engaged in the reverse process that leads from powerlessness to power. Men feel threatened at the prospect of self-emptying.

Yet by losing male privilege, men empower themselves humanly as they move from confrontation to encounter. By surrendering control, men grow in freedom. They enjoy closer relationships with women and learn to relish the joy that equal love brings. In social terms, men's power erodes; in personal terms, their love finds the footing that fulfills them.

How can men help in the liberation of women? They must first listen to women in a way that creates a new space for both men and women to inhabit. There are different ways of listening. It is all too easy for men to slip into a patronizing way of listening, or to listen only for what they want to hear. It is not easy to listen to anything that militates against an advantageous situation. A man genuinely listens when his own thoughts and feelings do not deafen him to what a woman is saying. It takes practice to listen to women with a view to discovering how they experience the world. Even if men disagree with women, at least by listening well they will be clearer about where they clash as well as converge.

But listening is only the beginning. Men need to respond, to ask questions, and to speak out of their own experience. Listening is not the end of the process but only the point of departure. Listening should lead to dialogue and to conversation. As well as by listening, men can help in the liberation of women by collaborating with them to change the way work is organized in our society. How can women combine being breadwinners and homemakers? Should women try to work only part-time? And will that mean exclusion from high-level jobs and no promotions? If women work full-time, who takes care of the children?

Women should be able to work in a way that at least partially reflects their difference from men, while simultaneously respecting their equality. Women tend toward cooperation instead of competition, they tend to use power not so much to control others as to make sure responsibility is shared, and they like to have time outside of work for family and raising children. But work and the workplace are currently structured to reflect men's preferences. What if we changed this? If the workplace were a setting where everyone was encouraged to be trusting, to pool resources, to not compete, and to serve instead of dominate, the world of work would be transformed. At present women are pressured to prove themselves by being overly ambitious, assertive, and competitive. It would be much better for all if they could be faithful to their compassionate and nurturing side. Women display great care within the home for their husbands and children. They are sensitized to the needs of their children. Mothers can interpret the cries of a little baby, and guess when it is hungry or tired or in pain. Mothers arrive in the workplace with this profound experience of nurturing and caring behind them. They are "tuned in" to relationships. Faced with a new client at work, they are inclined to ask, "How can I help this person?" instead of, "How can I make money from them?" If the structures of the working environment could encourage women to use their relational and nurturing skills, society would benefit immeasurably.

Women need a balanced working life, with time for activities outside work. If their preferences were taken seriously in Western societies, we would have a shorter working week and thus less take-home pay, but also happier and more fulfilled lives. In the male world of work, there is such an emphasis on work itself that all other interests get sidelined. Consequently, when men lose their jobs, it hits them much harder because they have no life outside of work to fall back upon. If men could release themselves from the pressure of feeling they have to work to prove themselves, they would lead less stressful lives and have more time to spend with their wives and children.

Men can help in the liberation of women by acknowledging that the issue is not just a women's issue. The truth is that it is an issue for everyone, women and men. It is a human issue. Furthermore, it is a human issue that does not stifle men, but frees them to be more human. Because more men in Western culture are getting their children up in the morning, bathing them, fixing them breakfast, and driving them to school, these men are becoming more caring, compassionate, and service-oriented in the workplace as well. These men have the wonderful privilege of nurturing essential human qualities that their own fathers and grandfathers were never expected to develop.

This is not to suggest that men are less loving or compassionate than women. Nonetheless, Western culture gives women greater permission to nurture and care, but is less accommodating with regard to men. Slowly and surely this situation is changing. More and more men are willing to share in the task of rearing their children. They want enough flexibility in their working hours to give time to their families. They know they can become more rounded people through developing their affective life, through prioritizing relationships over power, and through cooperating instead of competing. They do not want to miss out on friendships, the simple joys of life, and, most of all, love. They are beginning to realize that their biggest legacy to the world will not be the importance of their jobs or the size of their salaries, but the quality of their marriages and families and the affection with which their children hold them dear.

Christianity has often been accused of disempowering women. Although many Christian men have been less than just in their dealings with women, Christianity itself launched a new age for the women of the world: "There is no longer male and female; for all of you are one in Christ Jesus" (Gal 3:28). Jesus stood out through his positive treatment of women. Jesus reaffirmed the Jewish commandments of marital fidelity and the prohibition of adultery, thereby providing women with dignity, protection, and marital stability. He spoke to the Samaritan women at the well whom every other man ignored; while a guest at dinner, he allowed a woman known as a public sinner to wash his feet and dry them with her tears, even though his host Simon, a Pharisee, thoroughly disapproved; after the Resurrection, he rewarded women for their fidelity by appearing first to them, and only later to men. Faith in Jesus Christ has empowered generations of women, from Mary Magdalene to Catherine of Siena to Mother Teresa of Calcutta. Today's Church could do with a fiery and feisty Catherine of Siena to give some of its smug prelates a salutary kick up the backside, because unfortunately Christians have not always followed Jesus' good example when it comes to women. Nothing has thwarted the good intentions of Christ more than bad Christians. There are hopeful signs that Christian Churches are beginning to realize the importance of making space for women to participate more fully in leadership roles. But for all that, little has actually been done. Institutional change is slow.

Even though Christian institutions do not live up to the perfect example of Christ, Christianity is nevertheless a positive force for women. It takes a robust stand against practices that are tolerated in many cultures: Christianity is firmly against the stoning of women, the burning of widows, temporary marriages, and sexual slavery. Christianity has contributed to a more positive stance toward women. Indeed, as the West drifts away from Christian values, there is a new aggression against women. Women are becoming increasingly objectified, and the West is in danger of descending into a new age of barbarism in which women will lose the freedom Jesus brought them.

A former Irish prime minister, Garret Fitzgerald, is once reported to have said: "This sounds fine in practice, but what's it like in theory?" Christianity has always been better in theory than in practice. Christianity's theory, whatever its practice, stands out as a beacon of light for both women and men.

CHAPTER FIVE

Work to Become Yourself

> About the only thing that comes to us without
> effort is old age.
>
> Gloria Pitzer

Would you call someone a worker who makes millions on the
stock market in a few hours without producing anything for
society? What about the sharp-eyed businessman who sells
shares at an inflated price just before their value is about to
plummet? Work in the true sense of the word is not done by
speculators who prey on the weakness of others and who
exploit financial instability for private or corporate gain.

    Work should never exploit other human beings or nature.
Work should respect human beings, nature, and society, and
make something better of them. Work cultivates things so that
they will blossom even more. In the Book of Genesis, God settled Adam in the Garden of Eden to cultivate it. Adam's task
was not to dismantle the garden and sell it to the highest bid-
der (that would have been difficult in any case, since there was
no one else around), but to make it bloom into a better garden.

    Work is an activity that demands a considerable expendi-
ture of energy. Work changes things and produces a useful
result. It is not done for its own sake or the sake of enjoyment:
although the activity of work may itself be enjoyable, the goal is
not enjoyment but a useful result and a change in things. Work

is performed either to fulfill a need, such as earning one's livelihood, or to serve higher values, such as the case of a nurse who serves the sick, or a thinker who serves the truth. Work entails effort, sacrifice, and even pain. It is a victory not only over the chaos of the external world but also over the chaos of internal scatteredness and formlessness. Work is not instantaneous; it requires sustained application over a period of time. It is precisely because of the perseverance it demands that work can affect us so deeply and form us so well. By making things, we forge our own selves. Work is life's way of making something worthwhile out of us. Whereas animals repeat actions in an instinctive way, human work is creative and inventive.

> A spider conducts operations that resemble those of a weaver, and a bee puts to shame many an architect in the construction of her cells. But what distinguishes the worst architect from the best of bees is this, that the architect raises his structure in imagination before he erects it in reality. At the end of every labour-process we get a result that already existed in the imagination of the labourers at its commencement.[1]

For many in our world, *work* is a terrible four-letter word. Over 250 million children in the developing world miss out on childhood because they have to work—some are as young as five years of age. In Asia and Central America, many workers producing clothes in sweatshops do not receive enough wages for food, shelter, and basic subsistence. African factory workers in close contact with dangerous substances are refused protective equipment and forced to work in unventilated spaces; if they get sick, they are denied access to the company's medical services. The 250 million children worldwide who are forced to work have little or no say about their working conditions, how they work, and the goal for which they labor. This makes it difficult if not impossible for them to draw any satisfaction from their work. The more wealth they produce for others, the poorer their own existence seems by contrast. Their human world depreciates in inverse proportion to the increased value of products. Trapped in degrading jobs, workers themselves become reduced to commodities. They are treated as disposable products, as machines without dignity or feelings, whose destinies are to be decided by questions of profit and loss. Meanwhile, they produce clothes they will never wear, cars they will never drive, and medicines they will never take. They pour their physical and psychic energies into things from which they will never benefit, except for the derisory wages they are given at the end of the week. There is no room for personal input and creativity. Workers become strangers to themselves. With little money and less dignity, they lose control over their lives. They become suspicious of others, and feel that life itself is against them.

But given the right conditions, work can be experienced in a positive and creative way. Work enables us to transform the world from disorder to order, from *chaos* to *cosmos*, in imitation of the creative rhythm of God, who fashioned the universe from the formlessness of chaos into the beauty of cosmos, making it into an orderly and harmoniously functioning whole. Work furnishes us with a rhythm that gives life a sense of purpose. Work imposes order on the chaos inside us, offering us the grace of anchoring our interior being in a reassuring rhythm that imitates that of creation outside.

This awesome cosmos flourished before we ever came along. When Adam was placed in the Garden of Even, he found himself in the midst of a blossoming estate that preceded him. Work is like that: we have the privilege of enriching and transforming something that existed before us—our world. In work we are never alone: we always find ourselves in the context of a preexisting universe immeasurably bigger than ourselves. We have the honor of making this world more human.

God asked Adam to cultivate the Garden of Eden, not to exploit it. When we cultivate, we respect the world around us, what has been given us. When we exploit, we hold the world around us in contempt, and we try to make as much money as possible out of it. When we misuse the world, it is as though we wrongly imagine that we are the creators of the universe, and that it is up to us to do with it as we will. But none of us made the sun or the stars; on the contrary, we ourselves are made of stars! Without generations of stars coming together with the gas of the universe, there would have been no chemical elements to make the human body.

> When I look at your heavens, the work of your fingers,
>   the moon and the stars that you have established;
> what are human beings that you are mindful of them,
>   mortals that you care for them? (Ps 8:3–4)

The fundamental choice before us today in our work is whether to cooperate with the universe or fight against it. Do we want to destroy things in order to re-create them in our own image, or do we want to enhance what we have already received as a gift? When we reflect a moment, we realize that we cannot live purely by destroying. Even our most mundane actions—drinking a cup of coffee—would be impossible without the hard work of a whole host of persons, from coffee growers to merchants to truck drivers to supermarket employees. We live from the work of our contemporaries. We build on their contributions. We are also indebted to the work of our ancestors who have made our lives what they are. We will never succeed alone, but through supporting each other and cooperating in order to develop what we have already received, we will attain true greatness.

Fulfilling work in a constructive working environment can form us in a deep way and help us become more truly ourselves, enabling us to develop our potential and realize our gifts, transforming not only the world outside, but also our inner world. We find new energy through finding a way to communicate our unique gifts. Moreover, as we express these gifts, we discover new gifts we did not realize we possessed. When work nourishes our personal growth and development, it is a real joy, so much so that we are almost ready to work for free. The best paycheck of all is the heightened sense of inner worth and outer acceptance that we feel.

Even people who have so-called "jobs for life" can arrive at the office one morning and discover their services are no longer required because the company is pushing for ever-greater profits and ever-lower costs. To the company, it is one less on the payroll; to the person laid off, it is the loss of a whole world. Will you be able to find another job in an ailing economy? Will anyone want to buy the skills you have to offer? Will it be even possible to make ends meet with unemployment insurance? Will you be able to spend time in the shopping mall again without becoming totally frustrated at your lack of purchasing power? Living in Western culture, which promotes the consumerist principle that every wish can and should be satisfied immediately, and that supposes everyone has enough money to buy the latest gadgets, you feel excluded from this secular heaven.

But losing a job is not just losing a steady income, although that cannot be underestimated: it is the loss of purpose and structure in life. What do you do now with all those waking hours? Where do you go from Monday to Friday? Is there somewhere you can go outside your apartment or house without feeling you have to justify your presence there? How can you even begin to create a new structure and routine when all you feel inside is pain and helplessness?

Losing a job is also the loss of a circle of friends and colleagues: the jokes and repartee at coffee breaks, the simple human connectedness that makes life infinitely more worthwhile. It is the loss of self-worth: work gives us social standing and makes us feel that we are contributing something to society. When the door slams in your face, it feels like society is saying you have nothing worth contributing anymore. You have been shut out, and there seems no way back. It is the loss of independence: holding down a job and standing on your feet financially make you feel like an adult in an adult world. But when you lose your financial security, it is like losing part of what it means to be a grown-up. You become like a child again, forced to turn wherever you can for support.

The inability to secure employment is crippling for people of all ages. When teenagers graduate from high school and young adults from college, it is difficult for them to have to hear the message that society does not need their enthusiasm and their skills, their energy and their commitment. They have just emerged from the world of adolescence, but they find no entry into the world of adult duties and responsibilities. This is a huge dent in their confidence, a gigantic if unintended assault on their self-worth. For those who have held down a steady job for years, the experience of being laid off can be completely disorienting in a different way, because it is so unfamiliar and strange. They are thrown so much off balance that it is difficult for them to get up on their feet again. They feel like people bereaved. They go through denial, confusion, anger, and apathy. They lose their appetite, sleep irregularly, and spend hours staring vacantly at the TV or retreating into the shadowy world of the Internet. Their stress and frustration communicate themselves to those around them.

Work helps us express ourselves and become the persons we are meant to be. Unemployment is an evil because it denies us this crucial opportunity of self-realization.

The plight of the unemployed challenges us to rethink Western culture. Their plight challenges us to put human beings back at the center of society. Human beings, not profit, must come first. This is an insight that investors and business people do not readily see, but it is one they must learn to keep uppermost in their minds. If their policies lead to large-scale layoffs without any prospect of creating as many new jobs as they have gotten rid of, there is something seriously wrong with their conduct, because they have elevated profit above human beings.

The fact that human beings have priority in the realm of work is counterintuitive in today's world. We are inclined to think of work above all in economic terms. But if we learn to see that work is at the service of human beings, we will begin to envisage work in spiritual terms. Work creates character and forms the human spirit as nothing else can. The reverse is also true: the lack of work destroys the human spirit as few other things can.

When people lose their jobs and lose their incomes, they also lose their ability to participate in many of the activities our culture takes for granted: eating out, going to the movies, going on family outings and trips. The unemployed become steadily more isolated from the employed. If government gives tax breaks to the rich but scant support to the poor, it effectively divides the wealthy from the less fortunate, and further segregates society. Instead, it could take bold action to draw people together across the economic divide. If the welfare of the poor is not of equal concern to government as the well-being of the rich, an invisible ghetto is created. We may not see the walls, but they are there, thick, high, and difficult to surmount. In times of economic difficulty, nations become more divided through ignoring the weak and the vulnerable. On the other hand, nations become more cohesive and unified when they demonstrate to the weak and vulnerable how much they care. Government has a great opportunity to show it cares by implementing policies to help those who are poor and those who have become impoverished through layoffs.

One of the negative effects of unemployment on Western culture as a whole is that, over time, all of us, even the gainfully employed, learn to tolerate and accept it as though it were a natural and inevitable state of affairs. As we become accustomed to higher unemployment rates, our sense of righteous indignation gives way to a vague unease and finally to a sense of complacency. We begin to feel that a high level of unemployment is a regrettable but inevitable aspect of modern life. It is certainly true that technological developments have permanently done away with certain kinds of manual work. But at the same time, there are huge needs in Western culture that are not being tackled by the resources of labor, primarily because satisfying these needs does not generate enough profit. For instance, drug addicts need treatment, the disabled need assistance, and the environment needs care. We must question why our culture allows widespread unemployment when such urgent needs as these are not being properly addressed. The answer is linked to a false hierarchy of values: work is not organized around human beings, and human beings are not prioritized above profit. Profit is number one.

How can we help the unemployed return to the fold, find gainful employment, and attain a sense of self-worth? There are many straightforward ways. As citizens, we can help by electing politicians who give priority to the unemployed, by not transferring large sums of money outside the country in order to create profit at the expense of jobs at home, by paying our taxes, and by not agitating for tax cuts that will negatively affect the unemployed. As business leaders, we can help the unemployed by using our wealth and financial resources to create jobs where it is economically feasible, by not seeking to maximize short-term profits to the long-term detriment of workers, and by recognizing that we are not masters of our wealth, but only its stewards for the sake of the common good. As government, we can help the unemployed by doing our best to encourage the public and private sectors to give them jobs. Although jobs cannot be magically created out of thin air, government can nevertheless play a vital role in putting jobs at the top of the political and economic agenda. Furthermore, government can channel funds and subsidies into key job-creating industries so that these industries may expand and thrive to the benefit of all.

Hardly any unemployed person wants to be unemployed. Practically all want a job; and those who cannot find something worthwhile to do are willing to take on even menial jobs. The unemployed have a right to work; and every right has a parallel duty. Since the unemployed have a right to work, we have, at the very least, a duty not to interfere with their right to get a job. In certain cases, we are obliged by the even stronger duty to help them obtain their right to work.

We are all responsible for jobs—admittedly not equally responsible, because we do not all possess the same ability to help the unemployed. We vary in our powers and in our capacities. But whoever we are and whatever we can do, we should all be united in recognizing that unemployment is not so much an economic issue as a human problem of enormous gravity: it dehumanizes individuals, it damages the relations between persons and groups, and it destroys the very fabric of culture. We all need to work together to find creative solutions to this most pressing of problems.

In a period when people are desperate for any kind of work at all, it may seem insensitive to say a few words about our need for leisure. Many people cannot afford to even contemplate leisure: they are working simply to survive and are engaged in multiple jobs just to feed their families. They are working because they have to, and because they have to make ends meet. The last thing they want to hear about is the importance of interrupting work on a regular basis in order to take time off. But for all that, there is a deep wisdom in keeping the Sabbath day holy. It gives us a perspective on what ultimately matters and on where our priorities should be. The fast pace of work does not allow for the relaxed rhythm of meaningful conversations, friendships, the enjoyment of nature, and religious worship. The expectation of those who send us e-mails and text messages is that we will be available and responsive seven days a week: they have little understanding for someone who wants to be regularly unreachable. Yet by withdrawing once a week from the madness, we do ourselves physical and spiritual good.

Leisure is not the same as idleness. It is not about laziness and inertia, but about a receptive attitude that opens us to what is noble and good. We give time to friends and family, to community and to faith. We take time out, not in order to be proud of the work we have done (though this has its rightful place as well), but to be grateful for everything

we have received without earning it: above all, God's goodness to us. The Sabbath takes us beyond the logic of work
and reward, and introduces us to the mystery of God's gratuitous love for us, which does not have to be earned. Work
is a good thing. Love is much greater. God's love for us and
our love for God are utterly special. The highest priorities
are not the ones we create for ourselves, such as the work
we do. The highest priority is the one God commands: "You
shall love the Lord your God with all your heart, and with
all your soul, and with all your mind" (Matt 22:37). The true
expression of leisure is not inactivity, but the activity of loving God, the cultivation of wonder, prayer, and divine con-
templation. It is ultimately through recovering the spirit of
true worship that we will also be blessed with a free time
that ennobles us, so that we can in turn become more
humanized by our work.

CHAPTER SIX

It's the Environment, Stupid!

The ultimate test of a moral society is the kind of
world that it leaves to its children.

Dietrich Bonhoeffer

Recently I walked up Mount Vesuvius with a group of Irish
teenagers. We reached the top, made our way around the rim
of the crater, trudged over red dirt, and marveled at the gases
that rose up all around, as surreal as the steam that ascends
through manhole covers on the streets of Manhattan. After
pausing for a moment to take in the breathtaking sight of the
city of Naples stretched out beneath us, we whipped out our
cell phones and sent a barrage of text messages to friends
back in Dublin. Combining Mount Vesuvius with a fascinating guided tour to the ruined city of Pompeii the same day,
we returned to our hotel, glad to have had such a graphic
snapshot of the distant past. But when I read up on the volcano afterward, I discovered that it was not safely consigned
to history. In fact, the past of Vesuvius is rumbling menac-
ingly beneath the surface right now. It is a past that threat-
ens to invade our present, since this sleeping giant of a
volcano is not restfully asleep. It is a ticking time bomb. Ten
kilometers under the crater is a reservoir of molten rock, or
magma, that is 400 square kilometers large. Sooner or later
it is going to erupt.

A lot of us are coming to a similar realization about climate change. Something cataclysmic seems destined to invade our present and change our future, sooner rather than later. With every new scientific report, the possibility of catastrophe draws closer as the speed of change is continually revised upward: weather patterns are becoming increasingly extreme, glaciers are melting faster than we thought, more species than we anticipated are becoming extinct.

It is encouraging to see the rising public consciousness, the greater sensitivity to how we use energy and process waste, the push for radical action from political leaders, and the sight of big companies going green. Cutting greenhouse gas emissions is laudable, but it is not enough. We need to change much more than our external behavior; however, we may have to learn from some extremely painful experiences before we do. These experiences might just teach us the really profound meaning of order, purpose, and above all hope. Maybe as our world changes in a way that terrifies us, we ourselves will be transformed in a way that makes us better.

I am not claiming that we are facing the end of the world. Nobody knows when that will happen. Even if we think it is due soon, we need to remind ourselves that God's "soon" and our "soon" can differ by centuries or even eons. But in chapter 24 of the Gospel of Matthew, Jesus did predict some unpleasant world events for well before the end of the world. He also encouraged us not to be alarmed by them. "For nation will rise against nation, and kingdom against kingdom, and there will be famines and earthquakes in various places: all this is but the beginning of the birth pangs" (Matt 24:7–8).

Let us take just the issue of famine and ask what we might learn from famine on a large scale. Not merely famines somewhere else, in another part of the world, at a safe television-distance from ourselves, but on our own doorstep. This hypothesis is not so farfetched. In fact, the first warning signs of global hunger are already being played out in the sudden surges of temperature in the middle of winter that spur plants into bearing fruit, only for the fruit to be destroyed by the return of the normal cold. Another first sign is the severe and prolonged droughts that various countries are already experiencing. If harsh and long-running cold spells upset our summers and scorching heat derails our winters, if we suffer torrential rain during the dry season and drought during the rainy season, then we will face the kind of disorder that steadily leads to death. Animals will have nothing to feed on, and begin to starve. Human beings will most likely panic and kill whatever remaining animals there are for food, before turning desperately to birds and what will be left of the depleted fish stocks. It will be all too easy to find pretexts for war.

Many experts assert that we are to blame for these strange climatic patterns that could end up destroying much of life as we know it, including ourselves. I bow before their expertise, but I believe we are to blame in a deeper way than simply our abuse of resources. We have been to blame for centuries by the way we think and how we view the world, which has influenced the manner in which we have treated and mistreated it. Underlying all our behavior is a loss of a sense of the pattern and purpose of the universe.

We live in the disorder that exploits nature for profit, and undermines the sheltering pattern and harmonious rhythm of God's creation. Sooner or later, the nature we mistreat comes back to haunt us. In his poem "Der Erlkönig" (later set to music by Schubert), Germany's greatest writer, Goethe, tells the harrowing story of a father rushing his sick son home on a galloping horse through a dark forest. The father evokes the rationality of the Enlightenment. Like the self-confident

Enlightenment thinkers, he has banished the transcendent from his horizon: for this rational adult, the forest is simply a collection of trees, nothing more. But the world beyond reason will not be kept at bay. His son still has the innocence and wonder of youth, and hears the seductive voice of the elfin king whispering in his ears. The mysterious cry of nature breaks through. It has been rejected by rational people; now it takes its revenge in a deadly way. The elfin king, whose voice the father cannot hear, continues to invite the boy to another world. The child is frightened; the father becomes alarmed and kicks the horse into a swift gallop. But as the poem ends and the father arrives home, he discovers that his son is already dead in his arms: *"In seinen Armen das Kind war tot."*

This poem speaks to me of how the disorder of not respecting nature leads to death. God's creation in Genesis is characterized by order. God shapes the world into life from the random emptiness of chaos. God transforms chaos into order. Adam and Eve's sin once again introduces disorder, a disorder that directly affects creation. The very earth becomes cursed because of them, and plants that once brought forth fruit now only offer thistles and thorns.

I guess many Americans remember the slogan that Bill Clinton popularized during his successful 1992 presidential campaign: "It's the economy, stupid!" Through this simple refrain, Clinton convinced voters that George H. W. Bush had failed to address economic problems, and that he was the man to tackle them. The dominant issue in the West today appears to be the economy again, but it may just be the environment. If the environment does not work, neither will the economy. The depth and breadth of the environmental problems we face are staggering, and demand a staggering response. Climate change is having a major effect on our world, and will have an enormous, and still incalculable, impact on future generations.

We have to bring culture back into the ancient bond it once had with the earth, with nature: the English word *culture* comes from the Latin word *cultura*, which means "caring for the earth" or "cultivating the soil." Culture as we know it in the West is dependent for its sound functioning on the health of the natural world. If the world's climate goes crazy, our whole culture and way of life will be destroyed. The deteriorating state of our natural world calls us to make a major shift in our way of life. Up until recently, the assumption when it came to the environment was that it would willingly put up with any mistreatment we imposed upon it. It would continue to accept its lot with a brave face, be suitably deferential to us, and never for a moment question its unjust treatment. In any case, it was presumed to be so resilient that any exploitation of ours was highly unlikely to make a lasting mark upon it. It would bounce back sooner rather than later.

We have begun to see that our unquestioned assumptions about the natural world are in fact highly questionable. The natural world is not in great physical condition. If a suitably qualified medical team were to examine it, the members would no doubt prescribe uninterrupted rest and protection from human beings. The assumptions we have entertained about the environment for so long do not reflect reality at all. They reflect how we wanted the environment to behave. Now we are seeing how these assumptions benefited oil companies, automakers, airlines, and many of the giants of Western industry. But these assumptions are imperiling our common future.

One worrisome aspect of our concern for the environment is that it generally proceeds in fits and starts. We become engulfed by intense fear when massive volcanoes erupt or tsunamis devastate coastlines and countries. But when the memories of these disasters dim, many of us return to our high tolerance threshold for environmental disrespect. Fear is not a reliable force of motivation.

There are two classic ways of motivating individuals: one is by promising them something they want, and the other is by intimidating them with the prospect of something they fear. The latter type of motivation is ineffective in the long run. The fear of an environmental Armageddon is not a lasting motivating force; at most, it works temporarily. We can be shocked into awareness by fear, but fear is not enough to make us change for good. Fear is only a useful motivator when we are intent on providing a short-lived surge in motivation. For instance, a man does not stay faithful to his wife for forty years because he is afraid of punishment. True change works on the basis of attraction rather than repulsion. We change because we are drawn by something, not because we are afraid of it. We can be jolted out of apathy and inertia through fear. But we do not *remain* awake and vigilant because of fear. Spine-tingling depictions of environmental catastrophe can certainly captivate the collective imagination, but these depictions will not sustain any long-term change. If fear is the sole motivating force, then once its dramatic effects wear off, it generally proves counterproductive. No one wants to live forever in thrall to dread and intimidation. We can be initially swayed by dreadful images of environmental crisis. But before long, we will gravitate back to our original credo.

Although our concern for the environment is fitful and sporadic, the destruction of the environment is itself proceeding by leaps and bounds. It is not only increasing; it is accelerating. We are moving faster and faster toward environmental meltdown.

None of us made this world. It precedes us. We are born into it. Unfortunately, in practice we easily forget this and act as though this world were something *we* created. We do not see ourselves as children of the earth but as masters of it. This collective self-image has a huge impact on human behavior. If we see ourselves as the center of the universe, we presume we can do what we want with the world. Although Copernicus banished the belief that the earth was the center of the universe, it was only when the first images of earth were beamed back from space that Copernicus's theory became visibly real. For the first time in history, we saw ourselves from the viewpoint of the rest of the universe, and got an inkling of how small, insignificant, and recent we really are. But the message still has not hit home.

We are on this planet for a short period, but what we do in this brief stretch of time can have far-reaching repercussions. Do we want to enable future generations to continue to live fruitfully on our planet? If we do, we need to be aware of how interwoven our destiny is with that of our world; we need to act out of a disposition that respects the earth. The Jewish philosopher Hans Jonas (1903–93) argued in *The Imperative of Responsibility*[1] that our radically changed world situation demands a new ethics. Traditional ethics focused on relationships between human beings, and, moreover, human beings of the same historical epoch. Traditional ethics was shortsighted. It did not draw attention to planetary obligations; neither did it consider long-term consequences or responsibilities to future generations. But according to Jonas, if we want to assure our continued existence on earth, our ethics has to recognize that the repercussions of our actions extend far into the future. This new ethics must be animated by the following imperative: "Act so that the effects of your action are compatible with the permanence of genuine human life."[2] In other words, act in such a way that the effects of your actions do not destroy human lives in the future. Whatever we do now should not compromise the continuation of human life on earth. Whatever we do today should contribute to the well-being of the earth tomorrow, and of all that lives on it. We must care for the earth through what we do, because that way the earth will last longer and provide a home for future generations.

The scenario is analogous to physical health. If we wish to preserve our health, we ought to take care of ourselves and ensure that we do not abuse our own bodies. Similarly, if we wish to preserve the well-being of future generations, we should care for the earth and make sure we do not exploit it. Admittedly there is a crucial difference: if I take care of myself, I will enjoy good health in the future. But when it comes to minding the planet, I am not going to get anything out of it in the long-term future, since I will not be around for that. Why should I care for future generations? After all, they are not going to care about me. In fact, when we reflect a moment, we realize that parents find themselves in a similar position. They are responsible for their children, but their children are not necessarily responsible for them.

If we want to ensure a future for human beings, we need to envisage nature as our ally, and not as our enemy. We are not in a trade-union standoff with our planet. Our role is not to exploit it as much as possible. In fact, the awareness that the stakes are so high, that we could destroy our planet, may paradoxically spur us to preserve it.

If famine, earthquakes, wars, and disease do become our lot, then this world's existence, which now promises to stretch into an endless future, will suddenly appear shockingly brief.

Just as the sun shines on the just and the unjust, so these disasters will make no distinction between good and bad: many millions will be wiped out. Nations that today seem powerful and invincible will crumble into the dust. Ideologies and doctrines that deceive many will become brittle and hollow as they totter and fall. This calamitous situation will exact enormous human suffering ("...Rachel weeping for her children; she refused to be consoled, because they are no more" Matt 2:18), and yet also offer us the grace-filled opportunity to turn to God. Impending disaster has the uncanny effect of focusing the mind.

But some of us will not want to think of death, much less of God. We will still persist in ignoring the stark reality immediately before us. We often put something in front of us so as not to see the abyss, and then proceed to race recklessly into it. The French thinker Blaise Pascal reflected deeply upon these diversionary tactics. He did not condemn them outright, because he realized that in a twisted way, they testify to our greatness: there is at least something altruistic about searching for our happiness *outside* ourselves, even though we do so in the wrong place. These distracting decoys are a form of disorder: we put a false goal in front of our eyes to conceal the real one from ourselves.

In *Girlfriend in a Coma*, an end-of-the-world novel by the Canadian writer Douglas Coupland, the character Karen wakes up from a coma after seventeen years, and finds her fellow human beings in the disorder of anesthetized and passionless lives, where efficiency and technological gadgets cannot hide the underlying void: "Animals and plants exist and we envy them that. But in people it just doesn't look good."[3] In a more accomplished novel, *White Noise* by Don DeLillo, a kind of prequel to the end of the world, the character Murray enthuses about the order he finds on television, and his words could easily be adapted to many kinds of virtual reality:

> …it welcomes us into the grid, the network of little buzzing dots that make up the picture pattern. There is light, there is sound. I ask my students, "What more do you want?" Look at the wealth of data concealed in the grid, in the bright packaging, the jingles, the slice-of-life commercials, the products hurtling out of darkness, the coded messages and endless repetitions, like chants, like mantras. *"Coke is it, Coke is it, Coke is it."*[4]

Murray explains to his students that their purpose is to fit into capitalist society, nothing more, nothing less. He prepares them for the banalities of consumerism, boxing them into a packaged world where there are only surfaces and no depth. Anything to stave off the ultimate questions and inoculate them against their deeper selves.

The ultimate disorder of all is despair. This is precisely what we should avoid when it comes to focusing on our personal and planetary future. We need to cultivate hope, which is the longing to seek our happiness in a life that goes on forever. Hope does not find its anchor in our own resources, and it is just as well, for if things around us become worse than we can now imagine, we will have no strength of our own upon which to rely. Yet precisely at that moment we may dare to rely upon God with a purity of intention we never dreamed possible. For when we have tried everything else and failed, God who is first will become our last hope.

CHAPTER SEVEN

Caring for Our Health

If you can eat anything you want to, what's the
fun in eating anything you want to?

Tom Hanks

As a teenager, I never truly grasped that my body was created
by God. Irish Catholic culture readily conspired to keep me in
my ignorance, constantly saying negative things about the
body. The result was that I did not like my body at all. That is
why it never even entered my mind that God might possibly
have knitted "me together in my mother's womb" (Ps 139:13).
As the years pass by, I am steadily attaining a more balanced
view of my body. At the same time, I have no wish to go to the
other extreme, and obsess about having a perfect body. Taking
care of the body is not the highest value in life, and feeding it
is not something that should take up so much time that we
have little energy left for loving. "Therefore I tell you, do not
worry about your life, what you will eat or what you will drink,
or about your body, what you will wear" (Matt 6:25).

I mention the body in connection with the subject of
health. I am always struck by the fact that the one element
all the reported apparitions of the Virgin Mary share in common is a call to bodily penance. Like any good mother, she
instinctively realizes that making a god of our own bodies
leads not only to physical illness but also to spiritual ruin.

Because I did not like my body, it never really struck me that it was important to take care of it by eating properly, exercising well, and getting enough sleep. I would like to think that the next generation of Christians is different, but as a result of teaching at the main clerical university in Rome, which has students from over 130 different countries, I am beginning to have serious doubts about the matter.

Standing in front of a lecture hall of students at the Gregorian University, I sometimes ask them what a human person is, and they generally respond to the effect that each person is a composite of body and soul. I then ask them in what way their bodies play a role in learning. Even though they have just told me that the body is an essential part of the human person, they are at a loss as to how they experience education in a bodily way. Some students say it only happens between classes when they take a brisk walk or do some physical exercise. When I then point out the obvious to them—that they are looking at me, listening to me, and taking notes—it dawns upon them that they are using their bodies—eyes, ears, and hands—during the lecture.

Even when they begin to see what should have long been evident, many seminarians still look at me with a trace of suspicion in their eyes, as though by mentioning the body I had touched on an area that it is distinctly unorthodox and even faintly heretical. To allay their mounting suspicions and to hammer the message home even more, I turn to one of the central doctrines in Christianity: the incarnation. Once again they are taken aback when I state something obvious that they have never truly noticed: God, the infinite, eternal, and omnipotent one, takes on the fragile body of a crying child in a manger. I emphasize that this is no playacting, no game, no costume change, but God's complete assumption of a real human body. Of course, they have heard about the incarnation

a thousand times, but they have only made fitful and sometimes unreal connections between the incarnation and their
own lives. I can almost see the puzzlement on certain faces as
they take in the amazing reality: "Gosh, God took on a human
body, like mine; that makes the body sacred." While they are
still reeling from the shock of this new insight, and while their
minds are desperately at work trying to integrate all of this into
their old worldview, which is bursting at the seams in the
process, I pepper them with some simple but ultimately reveal-
ing questions:

"Do you ever attend Mass?" I ask, tongue-in-cheek.

"Of course we do!" they reply indignantly.

"Do you ever pay attention to what happens there?" I
ask, even more provocatively.

Now they are not so sure. Perhaps this a trick question of
some sort, so they are generally slow to respond. But sooner or
later most of them give at least a hesitant nod.

"What does the priest give you at Mass?" I continue.

"Communion."

"And what does he say when he gives it to you?"

This is when the light begins to go on.

"The body of Christ," they reply slowly. The insight is
finally hitting home.

I have one more question: "And what do you say when
you receive it?"

"Amen."

"Yes, you say 'Amen.'" Now I have them on the ropes,
and if they have not yet been hit with the sucker punch,
here it comes: "And as you all know, *Amen* means a whole-
hearted, full-*bodied* yes."

For years, these seminarians have not realized that the
central act of the Catholic faith, the Eucharist, is one in which
Jesus Christ gives himself, not as a vague force or indefinite

energy, but as a body. For years they have been saying "Amen" in an unthinking and often mechanical way. Most of them have hardly reflected upon what they are saying "Amen" to, and what it really signifies. Given the importance God assigns to the body, how can they have neglected the body, or dismissed it so glibly as dangerous and sinful? How can they have looked down on the flesh, when God himself has taken on a human body, not as an ornament or decoration, but as an integral part of his identity in Jesus Christ? How can they have so stubbornly ignored the truth of Scripture, which says: "Or do you not know that your body is a temple of the Holy Spirit within you, which you have from God, and that you are not your own?" (1 Cor 6:19).

James Joyce, even though he constantly fulminated against Catholicism, saw the importance of the body much more clearly than these seminarians do. His youthful masterpiece, *A Portrait of the Artist as a Young Man*, is a clear demonstration of the fact. The beginning of the novel portrays the infant Stephen, despite his tender age, already at work "organizing" the physical world around him. Joyce, despite the apparent chaos of later writings such as *Ulysses* and *Finnegan's Wake*, was always highly ordered beneath the surface disarray, and at the beginning of this quasi-autobiographical novel, he subtly and cleverly introduces one by one the different senses of the infant Stephen. At first Stephen *hears* his father recount a story about a "moocow that was coming down along the road." Next Stephen *sees* his father looking at him, and notices that his father has a "hairy face." Joyce then introduces us to *taste*, as Stephen remembers that the shopkeeper Betty Byrne sells sticks of lemon-flavored sweets. And finally the senses of *touch* and *smell* are introduced: "When you wet the bed, first it is warm then it gets cold. His mother put on the oilsheet.

That had the queer smell." And all this is only the first page of the novel![1]

There is a lot of discussion today about improving access to health care, and rightly so. Health care is not a luxury: you cannot postpone having a heart attack while you purchase health insurance. Citizens should not have to live in perpetual fear of becoming sick, and they should not have to avoid going to the doctor for fear of finding out they are ill. Health care is a human right for all. But let us not lay too much blame on health care systems, because the primary responsibility for our health lies with each of us. Medicine treats us when we are ill and can help us regain health, but its importance can be exaggerated. What really makes us healthy is a healthy lifestyle. By making better choices, we can reduce the risk of the principal causes of death—heart disease, lung disease, cancer, and strokes. It is certainly true that our health can be affected by factors over which we have little or no control: genetics, a car accident, polluted water, industrial waste, and so on. But we cause many of our own health problems by abusing and mistreating our bodies. This fact raises intriguing questions: If we played a role in making ourselves sick, are we obliged to play a bigger role in making ourselves well? Should society be obliged to pay for a health mess that we ourselves created, contributed to, or worsened?

The truth is, we cannot shift too much blame onto health professionals, because we are often our own worst enemies when it comes to our health. Diet is a major culprit: in the West we have become accustomed to eating enormous quantities of junk food. Diseases of the heart as well as diabetes and cancer are frequently caused by fast foods such as potato chips, hamburgers, candy, ice cream, and sugary drinks. The most common chronic disease in the United States is obesity. In fact, in tandem with the spread of Western-style junk food around the world, the West has exported obesity as well. The number of overweight people around the world is rising so fast there is now an epidemic of "globesity."

Incredible as it sounds, a combination of healthy diet and regular exercise can greatly decrease the risk of major life-threatening diseases. Exercise not only burns calories and detoxifies the body, but also slows down the aging process, reduces stress, and encourages the production of beta-endorphins, which have a calming effect on the body. Why then do doctors prescribe diet and exercise so little and drugs so much? Has it something to do with intense lobbying from pharmaceutical companies, or do physicians simply think that patients would not believe that better health could be so straightforward?

While the sanctions against smoking in the West amount to a virtual crusade, our societies are more ambivalent about alcohol abuse. I come from a country that has huge ambivalence when it comes to alcohol. Irish socializing often revolves around drinking, and Irish people happily give themselves permission to consider the culture of drinking as part of their national character. There is certainly more to social drinking than drinking alcohol itself. Gathering in the pub also offers the chance to nourish human and spiritual values: companionship, music, fun, a carefree and welcoming atmosphere, intimacy, relaxation, and even conversations of a religious nature. But Irish people also turn a blind eye to the addictive side of alcohol. Instead they look on drinking as an appealing and integral part of what makes them so loveable to other nations. They do not want to face the fact that alcoholism is a disease, and a potentially deadly one; they prefer to regard it as carefree Celtic mischief.

Seven years ago I decided to stop drinking alcohol completely. I was not a problem drinker at the time. Neither was I taken over by a holier-than-thou impulse that pushed me to a higher moral ground in order to look down on everyone else. In truth, I am not against alcohol, because in itself it is a good thing. In fact, I really miss a fine red wine with a celebratory dinner, a French apple brandy at Christmas, and an Irish coffee on Saint Patrick's Day. But the most difficult part of this sacrifice is coping with people who are bothered with my choice not to drink, sometimes interpreting it as a judgment or even as a personal affront. If I told them I only ate kosher, I would probably receive more sympathy and understanding.

So why did I give up alcohol? Simply because I felt called by God to give up this good thing called alcohol for the sake of an even higher good—the healing of those who are addicted and of those who suffer because someone close to them is an alcoholic. I have seen too many people struggle terribly because of alcoholism and drug addiction. I am no hero, but I felt I had to do something, and this is what I decided to do.

Is my sacrifice going to achieve much in the big scheme of things? I believe it can have amazing results, but not at all because of me. Only because I continually offer it to God so that its impact can be multiplied, just as Jesus multiplied the simple offering of the loaves and fishes (the only miracle of his to figure in all four Gospels). My sacrifice is pretty useless unless I raise it up in prayer to God. That is what I do, delighted to know that when it comes to arithmetic, God is much more interested in multiplication than in addition. I know God will use this little gesture of mine to do tremendous good.

Complete abstinence from alcohol is not for everyone, but it is high time for all Christians to rediscover the old-fashioned virtue of temperance. Growing up in Ireland, I used to associate mortification and temperance with pain, sadness, and even depression. But now I have come to see that temperance does not reduce my enjoyment of life, but paradoxically increases it. After all, who really gets pleasure from the third slice of Black Forest cake? Or the twentieth cigarette? If we become dependent or even addicted to food and drink, we no longer enjoy them freely, because we simply cannot do without them. Going overboard when it comes to food and alcohol only enslaves us. Temperance, on the other hand, enables us to get greater pleasure from life.

But as well as the joy it brings, temperance is also physically strengthening, keeping the body younger and healthier. Leaving dinner with a little hunger inside is much better for our health than hauling ourselves up from the table bloated and sluggish. It can also serve as a salutary reminder of those who are truly hungry, and encourage us to be generous toward them.

The most mortified-looking people in today's Western world are well-to-do women. Many of them are pencil-thin, as though they were practicing mortification to perfection. On the other hand, on the basis of visual evidence, many overweight Catholic clerics look like they have never even heard of penance. But one of the best ways to ensure physical and mental equilibrium is to practice a little mortification through being moderate in what we eat and drink, and in all our natural needs.

The quality of our health is dependent on many of the topics we are exploring in this book. A healthy society is shaped by healthy families. The health of a nation is enhanced by a liberating balance between work and leisure. Environmental factors such as the pollution of the atmosphere, the land, and the water, all undermine health. A nourishing spirituality contributes to physical health. It is already demanding enough for doctors to care for the body. It is too much to expect that they should also be physicians of the soul, and our salvation as well. But while not expecting too much from doctors, we should not isolate physical health from considerations of our wider well-being. We should care for ourselves in a holistic way. We should tap all our energies and seek to realize ourselves in a full way.

CHAPTER EIGHT

War Is Awful

I know war as few other men now living know it, and nothing to me is more revolting. I have long advocated its complete abolition, as its very destructiveness on both friend and foe has rendered it useless as a method of settling international disputes.

General Douglas MacArthur

In the Hebrew mind, words were regarded as so powerful that they could bring about what they uttered. Words released a primal energy from the person that, once spoken, could not be taken back or revoked. The power of human words was seen as mirroring the power of the word of God:

For as the rain and the snow come down from
    heaven,
  and do not return there until they have
    watered the earth,
making it bring forth and sprout,
  giving seed to the sower and bread to the eater,
so shall my word be that goes out from my mouth;
  it shall not return to me empty,
but it shall accomplish that which I purpose,
  and succeed in the thing for which I sent it.

(Isa 55:10–11)

The word of God enters the very being of the prophets, setting them on fire and giving them something of God's own unbounded energy. When Jeremiah receives God's word, he is consumed by an inner fire he cannot put out. Ezekiel eats the scroll upon which God's word is written, and the scroll tastes as sweet as honey. The fact that Jesus Christ is called the *Word* of God is an unmistakable sign of how utterly special words are. Every word is a gift of God. Words can have an irresistible energy and can transform our lives for the good. But if we abuse these gifts of God, words can cause evil.

Harmful words can lead to aggression, violence, and war. A sociologist called William Brennan has convincingly shown just how destructive language can be. Brennan looked at seven different targets of victimization: Native Americans, African Americans, Soviet enemies under communism, European Jews and others exterminated during the Holocaust, women, the unborn, and the disabled and/or dependent. In each case, he provided firsthand documentation to demonstrate that each of these vulnerable groups was attacked verbally, which in turn justified brutal and violent behavior.

Despite the enormous variety of victims of verbal and physical violence, Brennan argued that all instances of destructive name-calling fall under one or other of these eight categories:

> *deficient human* ("stupid," "defective," "inferior,"
> "potential life," "lives not worth living"), *less than
> human* ("subhuman" and "nonhuman"), *animal*
> ("beast" and "lower animal"), *parasitic creature*
> ("parasite," "vermin," "lice"), *infectious disease*
> ("pestilence," "plague," "epidemic," "infection,"
> "contagion"), *inanimate object* ("thing," "prop-
> erty," "material," "merchandise"), *waste product*

("trash," "rubbish," "debris," "garbage," "refuse"),
and *nonperson* (social, psychological, or legal
nonexistence).[1]

Brennan's study flatly contradicts the childhood chant:
"Sticks and stones may break my bones, but words will never
hurt me." Our words influence our actions. Disparaging
words practically offer excuses for acts of oppression and
violence. If we look on the elderly as humanly deficient,
their lives will not seem worth cherishing or even preserv-
ing. If we describe gypsies as non-human or animal, we will
feel entitled to treat them in a non-human way, to treat
them like animals. If we see illegal immigrants as parasites,
debilitating in their effects upon us, robbing our space, and
impeding our proper functioning, we may just feel entitled
to send them back to certain persecution in their countries
of origin. If we regard the unborn as waste products, we will
want to clear them away. If we think of Islam as a disease,
we will avoid it for fear of becoming contaminated, and try
to keep it as far away as possible in order to remain cultur-
ally healthy. If women are viewed practically as inanimate
objects, men will readily objectify them, and feel little guilt
in treating them badly. If the disabled are not considered to
have the legal status of personhood, this can legitimize total
neglect of them.

How do we reverse linguistic violence when the human
tongue has no backspace key? How do we go beyond name-
calling when the best technology cannot take back a word
already spoken in anger? We need to become aware of the
potentially catastrophic influence of the words we speak,
and remember at the same time that the nasty words we
swallow before uttering them can do no harm. It is easy to
forget that words have consequences, and that negative

words can have disastrous repercussions. When a culture becomes used to dehumanizing labels, it begins to mindlessly accept the falsehood of degrading epithets as the truth. But the unkind things we refrain from saying never harm others or ourselves. Awareness is a key factor. If we become alive to the destructive potential of language, we will watch over the negative thoughts that are constantly threatening to become words, and we will be quick to challenge dehumanizing labels. We will pay attention to how our culture uses language, and take a stand against victimizing labels. As well as challenging a violent vocabulary, we also need to cultivate a positive lexicon, words that affirm and enhance human dignity. We need to reinstate a humane and dignified vocabulary to describe all human beings.

We also need to examine carefully the words that Western culture speaks to *us*. Are they true words? Do they enrich our lives? Do they humanize or dehumanize us? Do they open our hearts or make us more narcissistic? Do they invite us to greater freedom or instead suppress crucial layers of our humanity? A nourishing culture invites us to create and inhabit a liberating language. The power of words is so great that we are in serious danger of becoming what we say.

We need to pause in order to examine the words we use without a second thought. In their book *Metaphors We Live By*, George Lakoff and Mark Johnson have shown how our everyday speech is peppered with metaphors that shape the way we understand reality, although we are largely unconscious of the influence these metaphors exert upon us. Without even being aware of it, we use a host of warlike metaphors when we get into arguments. Lakoff and Johnson give these examples:

> Your claims are *indefensible*.
> He *attacked* every weak point in my argument.

His criticisms were right on *target*.
I *demolished* his argument.
I've never *won* an argument with him.
You disagree? Okay, *shoot!*
If you use that *strategy*, he'll *wipe you out*.
He *shot down* all of my arguments.[2]

It is not just that we use military metaphors in our arguments; it goes much further than that. The language we use determines our conduct so that the arguments themselves can easily degenerate into downright belligerence. We practically interact with our opponents as we would with enemies, attacking their positions, trying to gain ground on them, and changing our line of defense when necessary in order to make our arguments as bulletproof as possible. This is so normal and so taken for granted that it does not even strike us as worth reflecting upon. It is difficult to see how much our words influence our thinking and behavior unless we picture a culture where arguments would not be envisaged in such a conflict-ridden way.

Imagine a culture where an argument is viewed as a dance, the participants are seen as performers, and the goal is to perform in a balanced and aesthetically pleasing way. In such a culture, people would view arguments differently, experience them differently, carry them out differently, and talk about them differently. But we would probably not view them as arguing at all: they would simply be doing something different. It would seem strange even to call what they were doing "arguing." Perhaps the most neutral way of describing this difference between their culture and ours would be to say that we have a dis-

course form structured in terms of battle and they
have one structured in terms of dance.[3]

If we incessantly interact using warlike metaphors,
isn't it possible and even likely that our arguments and dis-
agreements will be aggressive and divisive, so that the way
we speak will not only influence how we behave, but also
shape our culture in ways we never consciously planned or
anticipated? Bellicose metaphors can give us permission to
behave in ways we would never have dreamed of in their
absence. Arguments are not of their nature like wars; but by
virtue of the metaphors we use, we make them appear in
this antagonistic light. If we see arguments in terms of war,
we can find ourselves practically sanctioning warlike conduct toward fellow human beings. Metaphors can almost
decide how we think about things. We tend to see reality in
ways that confirm the metaphors we have, and not in ways
that challenge or deny these metaphors.

Even apart from questions of language, our culture is
excessively fixated on war. As the French writer Blaise
Pascal once observed, can anything be sillier than the fact
that the man on the other side of the river has the right to
kill me simply because his ruler has fallen out with mine,
even though I have no bone to pick with this man? Many of
us would like to believe that human beings are basically
good, genuinely interested in the welfare of others, and
most reluctant to harm them; therefore we prefer to blame
war on the machinations of corrupt leaders or the influence
of bad institutions and social structures that maneuver well-
meaning individuals into doing all sorts of reprehensible
things. But no human being is an angel, and in our more
clear-headed moments we have to admit that each of us has
felt at least at one time or another (and more likely too many

times for our own comfort) a thirst for power and an urge to control others irrespective of their wishes. In other words, the witness of our own lives and the witness of history (100 million human beings killed by their fellows in the course of the twentieth century) together conspire to show that we are evil as well as good, corrupt as well as noble.

War is a grave matter with terrible consequences, and never something to be entered into lightly. No war is good or glorious; every war is painful and regrettable, even when a nation feels war is the morally unavoidable thing to do. That is why responsible leaders seek to resolve conflict by peaceful means first. Only when all viable alternatives have failed do they turn to force. They do not go to war to distract attention from flagging economies or to boost electoral prospects; they do not attack other countries for the purpose of gaining new territories or amassing greater wealth. They go to war only as a response to serious aggression. They do not run the risk of sending in troops if there is no prospect of success. And if they do decide to attack, they are careful not to cause more destruction and damage with their own weapons than the damage caused by the aggressor they are trying to defeat.

The most sophisticated weapons in the world are not enough to make us secure against war. It is our way of life that best protects us from overt hostility. A society that lives in a peaceful way will not want to go to war in the first place, and will be more likely to halt an enemy through negotiating instead of stubbornly refusing to talk. Although people give all sorts of noble reasons for going to war, armed conflict quickly degenerates into hatred. Now, hatred is a strong word to use, and being capable of hatred is not a pleasant quality to ascribe to anyone; but if love is seeking the well-being of others, the least that can be said of a soldier pounding your house with artillery shells is that he is not full of benevolent feelings in your regard. Another way of putting this is to say that this soldier hates you. He may claim he is trying to liberate you and secure your freedom, but if you are in serious danger of dying first, this claim rings hollow. Hatred does not like to reveal itself as such, so it puts on respectable masks like national security, self-defense, and patriotism.

Fear of other people is often at the root of war. Islamic terrorists are afraid of what the West will do to their religion and culture. We Westerners are afraid of what these terrorists want to do to us and our world. Israelis are afraid that millions in the Arab world may want to wipe them off the map. Millions in the Arab world are afraid because Israel has the military capability to inflict terrible damage upon them.

No state is intimidated by a weaker one, but every nation is afraid of a more powerful neighbor. Just like individuals always want to keep up with the Joneses, a nation will find it hard to resist the temptation to buy the latest military gadgets to compete with its stronger neighbor. Getting caught up in an arms race out of international envy can be a needless waste of money, for a state may in fact be already sufficiently strong and secure from a military point of view. But however strong it actually is, if it discovers that another nation is even stronger, it will inevitably feel uneasy. Unfortunately this leads to a vicious circle: one nation arms to feel safer, and the neighboring state misinterprets this as a preparation for war, and produces even more weapons in response. The result is that neither state feels secure: both end up with an even greater sense of vulnerability, along with a hefty military budget.

The poorest countries cannot start wars because they lack the economic and military resources to do so. Nations that have moderate resources but feel deprived relative to richer nations are likely candidates for war. They want things they cannot get, and they are willing to engage in conflict to acquire what they feel is rightfully theirs. Not only the relative standard of living, but also the nature of an economic system can be a determining factor when it comes to war. Free market economies are likely to avoid war to the extent that it damages trade, undermines their profits, and drains them of the resources they need for business.

The political system of a given society plays a decisive role as well. Democracies are accustomed to resolving conflict through discussion and dialogue, and, interestingly, democracies hardly ever engage in war with other democracies, but mostly with rogue states or dictatorships. Furthermore, the very structure of democracy makes it more pacific in nature. Government is accountable to the people, and all citizens have fundamental rights that the state cannot take away. One of these rights is that citizens can make their opinions heard, and if they feel war is wrong, they will say so. However, even democracies can manipulate the public so that they become inured to a culture of violence and war. And although democracies do not resort to war with fellow democracies, they do intervene militarily in order to spread democracies throughout the world.

There are many questions that need to be posed before a country resorts to war. And there are few easy answers. First of all, is there a legitimate authority to approve war? Apart from instances of self-defense, international law grants the UN the sole right to authorize war. This situation is not ideal, since there is a widespread crisis of confidence in the UN today. Yet while it is undoubtedly a flawed institution, it still works. The best way forward is not to ignore the UN and to refuse to acknowledge its authority, but to continue to cooperate with it while simultaneously working to reform it, so as to make it less cumbersome and less unfocused, and more effective and more accountable. Right now, powerful nations either push through their own agendas at the UN, or failing this, are tempted to act independently of it. The UN is no longer perceived as effective, impartial, representative, or transparent. If the five permanent members of the UN Security Council who wield veto power—the United States, China, Russia, the United Kingdom, and France—do not move to reestablish the integrity of the UN, this institution founded in 1945 will continue to lose international confidence.

There are many disputed issues around the question of just war. Those of a pacifist leaning claim that a country should wait until it is attacked before thinking of going to war. The more hawkish contend that if there is a perceived threat, it should not hesitate to take preemptive military action. But it is difficult to gage the seriousness of a perceived threat, and how likely war is to transpire. If the threat is against the inhabitants of a third country, there will undoubtedly be reluctance to interfere in the internal affairs of another sovereign state. If war is a last resort, it is hard to judge how long to wait before waging it, and how much negotiation should precede it. If one party is not sincere about discussions but only is buying time to build up its military strength, waiting too long runs the risk of leading to higher casualties.

Once a nation commits itself to war, it is not easy to keep a just goal in mind, given the temptation to wage war out of hatred of an enemy instead of a desire for peace. The goal of the war may be good, but a nation can quickly degenerate into resorting to *any* means to attain its just end. Consequently, the havoc caused by war can end up outweighing the good being sought. World War II caused unprecedented destruction, yet most people would agree that the good achieved—the defeat of Nazi Germany—was worth the enormous human cost. But as a rule, it is not realistic to presume we can predict the consequences of war. On the one hand, war today is so inherently destructive that the use of military force seems always immoral. But on the other hand, the makers of highly sophisticated weapons and state-of-the-art intelligence capabilities claim that the use of force is more precise than ever before. Whatever the truth about this claim, civilian casualties are nearly impossible to avoid. But if civilian casualties are acknowledged as inevitable, they are not just tolerated, but arguably even "intended"; and by tolerating a high level of civilian casualties among the enemy in return for securing peace for ourselves, we are effectively deciding that their lives are less valuable than the lives of our citizens. This may be understandable, but does that make it right?

Let us not forget the soldiers who, when all is said and done, have the unenviable task of fighting our wars. I believe political leaders have an obligation to tell these soldiers face-to-face and in all honesty whether the cause they will fight for is worth dying for. The ultimate test of the leaders' sincerity would be either to fight alongside these soldiers or else to allow their loved ones to be deployed in the front lines as well. It is imperative that, for their part, soldiers view their enemies as human beings, as men (mostly) like themselves who also have mothers and fathers, brothers and sisters, wives and children. This humane vision will prevent them degenerating from disciplined soldiers into cold-blooded killers. It will help them retain moral ideals as well as displaying physical courage; it will ensure that their way of waging war will not become so brutal so as to destroy the last vestiges of their own humanity. When war has ended, a nation must ensure that its soldiers are welcomed home as heroes and not as villains. It must help them in the phase of transition so that they become morally well-adjusted members of society.

When war is finished, a just peace does not miraculously unfold. In fact, in many ways, war is not a realistic foundation for peace in the first place, since the use of arms generally promotes even more violence. In addition, victors are always tempted to exact revenge on the vanquished. They are not necessarily keen to respect the human rights and liberties of the defeated party. They do not always take adequate measures to prevent the defeated nation from descending into anarchy or civil war. Neither do they give serious thought to bringing it in from the cold, and reinserting it into the international community. It demands a generous imagination to think beyond the binary opposition of victory and defeat and instead envisage a new order of justice for all, one in which war itself hopefully will be no more.

CHAPTER NINE

Cultivating the Imagination

We do not need magic to transform our world. We carry all the power we need inside ourselves already. We have the power to imagine better.

J. K. Rowling

When I first entered the Jesuits, our novice master invited a gifted film critic to take our group occasionally to the movie theater in order to see nourishing and thought-provoking foreign-language films. I felt I was being introduced into a cosmopolitan world far more expansive and exciting than the village certainties to which I was accustomed. Yet I was not completely at home in this new world. For that reason I identified with the lead character in one of the films we went to see, *Pauline at the Beach* (*Pauline à la plage*), a charming French comedy that tells the story of an August vacation at a seaside resort in Normandy. Like the young Pauline, the teenage title character of the movie, I was unsophisticated and sincere. In the course of this beguiling French film, which is short on drama but long on dialogue, Pauline watches adults talk in exalted ways about love, yet all the while deceive themselves about its true nature. I found myself in a similar position: I was watching films made by cinematically sophisticated directors, yet just like the adults in the film *Pauline at the Beach*, these artists were not always as rich in human insight as they liked to imagine. But unlike Pauline in her coming-of-age film, I was too impressionable to trust my own misgivings about the art-house films our group went to see. I had a certain youthful wisdom, yet I had not enough self-confidence to believe in myself.

Well, that is, not until one evening when our film critic got so carried away that he brought us to see a film that none of us in his right mind would have freely chosen to watch. It was a somewhat abbreviated version of an epic Italian movie that had originally been released several years previously; but even this supposedly short version went on for four hours. I was eighteen years old and this was the most shocking film I had ever seen; and today I can add—have ever seen. Our group decided afterward to part company with this overzealous film critic. But images do not leave your soul as quickly: thirty years later I am still traumatized by one scene of sickening violence where a villainous Fascist murders a young boy. The scene lasted less than a minute, but unfortunately I can still picture this scene as vividly as if it had lasted an eternity and unfolded only yesterday. It is a poison that insinuated itself into my heart three decades ago, but even now, all these years later, I cannot expel it.

That early and harrowing cinematic lesson taught me the importance of cultivating the imagination with care. Imagination is a great gift of God that enables us to discern many layers of reality within and beyond the here and now. With the help of the imagination, we can see that this world is created in God's image; we can remind ourselves that God is good at every moment, not only those when something good happens to us. With the help of the imagination, we can picture Jesus at our side, and see everything through his eyes….

We need to protect this creative gift that helps us see real things that are not right in front of us, or not yet here.

Protecting the imagination means keeping vigil at its gateway. Western culture still realizes the importance of guarding the imagination: parents guard their children from racist words and images, because they know such words and images could lead to racist actions; Jewish people are justifiably concerned about anti-Semitic literature, because they know all too well from bitter historical experience that hateful words can lead to murderous deeds. Words and images can shape and misshape behavior when it comes to issues like racism. Western culture does not always want to see the link between violent words and violent conduct, or between sexually demeaning images and sexually demeaning deeds. Therefore, it is up to each of us to refuse to allow trash into our souls. Certain Christians have made such a stand by giving up on things such as television. They no longer allow complete strangers free entry into their living rooms in order to lie, steal, and murder on the screen before them.

We must not let just anyone kidnap our imagination and channel it into gratuitous sex and violence, or, for that matter, into trivialities. The acclaimed American novelist Jonathan Franzen remarked in an interview that a really difficult era forces us not to abandon old wisdom, but to preserve it, so that curiously "the day comes when the truly subversive is in some measure conservative."[1] We are living precisely in this kind of age, when we demonstrate our revolutionary grit by conserving what is best in tradition.

Imagination is at the heart of the Jesuit tradition. The Jesuits were founded by a man whose imagination was touched in a deep way by God. But the imagination of Ignatius of Loyola (1491–1556) could easily have propelled him in a self-centered direction, for his imagination had been shaped not just by his Christian upbringing, but also by his short-lived career as an ambitious, swashbuckling soldier. Ignatius was thoroughly chivalrous and also remarkably stubborn, which is why in 1521 he persuaded a small band of Spanish soldiers to defend the walled city of Pamplona against a French army that outnumbered them by a ratio of more than twelve to one. Not surprisingly, this foolish act of bravery ended in complete defeat, and Ignatius himself was hit by a cannonball that shattered his right knee. He was taken back to his family home in the Basque country of Spain and underwent repeated operations to straighten his leg. As a result he spent nine months lying in bed. If Ignatius had lived in our own day, he probably would have turned on his laptop and played endless high-octane video games. But in the sixteenth century, all he could do was turn to books.

He wanted to read stories of warriors and romance, but the only reading material in the house was about the life of Jesus and the lives of the saints. The book that especially touched Ignatius was the *Life of Christ*, written by Ludolph of Saxony, a fourteenth-century Carthusian monk from Germany. What distinguishes this book is the huge role it gives to the imagination. Ludolph summons his readers to enter imaginatively into the Gospel scenes he describes, by seeing and hearing these events as though they were unfolding before readers in the present moment, and then by inserting themselves into these scenes, becoming one or other of the characters who witness a miracle of Jesus or the suffering of his passion. Ignatius was so taken by Ludolph's approach that he copied down three hundred pages of notes from the *Life of Christ* while convalescing. Aristotle long ago pointed out that we learn by imitating others, and Ignatius began to learn a new rhythm of being as he "tasted" deeply these scenes from the life of Jesus. But these were not the only images to grab his attention. Whenever he placed his devotional reading to one side, his thoughts wandered back to chivalrous adventures.

During that long summer of 1521, two sets of images competed for his loyalty: on the one hand, visions of spiritual virtue and saintly heroism; on the other, dreams of derring-do and high-society romance. After a while, Ignatius came to a valuable insight: he noticed that the prospect of becoming a knight in shining armor gave him a real thrill while he thought about it, yet later left him feeling empty. But the episodes from the life of Jesus not only brought him consolation while he pictured them; they also left him with a sense of contentment that lingered long afterward. What made Ludolph of Saxony's *Life of Christ* even more effective in shaping Ignatius was the fact that it shared key features with the best chivalrous tales: it had an epic sweep, was action-packed, and issued a call to service. Because Ludolph's narrative was so courtly and valiant in nature, it was guaranteed to appeal to a would-be knight. Ignatius discovered that God was speaking to him strongly through these scenes in which he imaginatively participated, while a less-welcome voice was speaking to him through his self-seeking daydreams. It began to dawn upon him that his imagination was a zone of conflicting spiritual forces. When his imagination followed God's call, he felt happy and content; when his imagination brought to life his knightly ambitions, he was left restless and ill at ease. Unlike me, Ignatius never went to the movies, but if he had, I am sure he would have been a cinemagoer with a difference, paying attention most of all, not to the content of films, but to the different emotions and moods they generated inside him.

Ignatius realized that he could waste his imagination through idle daydreaming, filling it with fantasies and illusions—or he could employ his imagination in an intentional way in order to envisage and catch hold of loving possibilities, and see and inhabit the world in a more selfless way.

On the one hand, he could remain passive and allow the surrounding culture of chivalrous romance to imagine his life away for him; on the other hand, he could take active hold of his imagination, and invite God to imagine his life with him in a way worthy of a child of God.

A similar choice faces us when it comes to reading, watching television, or surfing the Internet. We can waste our time on superficialities and gossip; we can damage our souls by exposing ourselves to bad reading and harmful images. Or we can choose uplifting material and helpful images, and read stories of people worth imitating.

If we do not take the trouble to develop our imagination, the surrounding culture will imagine our lives for us, focusing our attention on things like sex, money, clothes, and gadgets. Physical and material things promise immediate gratification, whereas it takes more time and effort to place ourselves imaginatively into a gospel scene. The more we become distracted by immediacies, the more we begin to wonder whether there is a world beyond the senses. When we fill our minds only with what we can see, hear, touch, taste and smell, the tangible and visible world becomes everything for us. We begin to doubt values we cannot touch or feel, like goodness and truthfulness, and invisible realities like God and the soul become steadily less real. While God's grace can enlarge our imagination, a superficial culture can lead to a shrunken imagination.

Literature expands our imaginative horizons when we enter into the experience of others and empathize with them. The canonical works in music, art, and literature are capable of unveiling new worlds for us. But it is also salutary to remember that the catharsis of emotion released by a work of art does not necessarily lead to a better society: well-dressed theater-goers in London's West End may cry copiously at the plight of Jean Valjean in the musical *Les*

Misérables, only to ignore the homeless man who begs for spare change in the street outside.

Art and literature do not automatically make us better people. The Holocaust happened in one of the most ostensibly civilized societies of Europe. *Cultured* human beings had few scruples in instigating and sustaining murder on an unimaginably vast scale. In the words of George Steiner:

> We know now that a man can read Goethe or Rilke in the evening, that he can play Bach and Schubert, and go to his day's work at Auschwitz in the morning. To say that he has read them without understanding or that his ear is gross, is cant. In what way does this knowledge bear on literature and society, on the hope, grown almost axiomatic from the time of Plato to that of Matthew Arnold, that culture is a humanising force, that the energies of the spirit are transferable to those of conduct?[2]

Auschwitz continues to be a formidable challenge for culture. Theodor Adorno famously said that to write a poem after Auschwitz would be an act of barbarism. According to Adorno, in the wake of the unspeakable treatment meted out to Jews in this extermination camp, poetry was no longer possible. Adorno's view is provocative, but I beg to differ. In the wake of the Holocaust, poetry is perhaps the most appropriate and urgent expression of all, for it can express what is deepest in the human being.

Maybe we should not interpret Adorno too literally. We could reformulate his statement as follows: "In the wake of Auschwitz, we dare not treat culture as glibly as we did beforehand, as though nothing had happened in the interim." Auschwitz brutally exposed the failings of high European culture. It calls to mind the hellishness into which human beings can still descend. Horror has not left us: we still live in the shadow of wars, global terrorism, and a steadily disintegrating environment.

We can learn a lot about renewing our world through reflecting upon great works of art. Wolfgang Amadeus Mozart's opera *Don Giovanni*, which premiered in Prague in 1787, is an education in love and its counterfeits, truth and falsehood, and the nature of freedom. I first got excited about this opera through reading what the Danish philosopher Søren Kierkegaard had to say about it. Kierkegaard has often been labeled the "melancholy Dane" (and not entirely without reason), but he was utterly effusive in his praise of *Don Giovanni*, and his brilliant analysis of Mozart's masterpiece is itself a work of genius. Here is Kierkegaard's description of the opening overture:

> It is powerful like a god's idea, turbulent like a world's life, harrowing in its earnestness, palpitating in its desire, crushing in its terrible wrath, animating in its full-blooded joy; it is hollow-toned in its judgement, shrill in its lust; it is ponderous, ceremonious in its awe-inspiring dignity; it is stirring, flaring, dancing in its delight.[3]

I am staggered at how Kierkegaard's original description in Danish often perfectly matches the tempo and rhythm of the opera. I am even more amazed because he never had the opportunity to listen to recordings of *Don Giovanni*: the gramophone was invented over thirty years after Kierkegaard's death. However, *Don Giovanni* was frequently performed in Copenhagen during Kierkegaard's lifetime (1813–55), and excerpts were regularly performed at concerts.

The protagonist of Mozart's opera, the eponymous Don Giovanni, represents a new departure in opera inasmuch as he is the villain of the piece. Until Mozart turned things on their head, it had been customary to choose a hero as the lead character in opera. But Don Giovanni is a villain, and a most charming one at that. He seduces the audience as successfully as he seems to seduce every woman he encounters.

Mozart is of two minds about Don Giovanni, and that is why the music elevates this philandering aristocrat and berates him at the same time. The subtitle of the opera is *dramma giocosa*, at once suggesting its serious and comic aspects. The opening overture confirms this impression, starting out solemnly in the key of D minor, before yielding to the merriment and life of the corresponding major key.

Don Giovanni, rich, privileged, and oozing with charm, is free to follow his instincts without restraint. As soon as one woman is conquered, he is already seeking the next. Yet following his instincts also makes him radically unfree: he is addicted to seduction. And so the questions: Is freedom meant for the sake of becoming enslaved to every appetite that stirs inside? Is freedom meant for the sake of endless consumption? Is freedom meant for the merely private in life? Or is it meant for something higher than self-indulgence and something wider than the narrowness of an exclusively personal agenda? In fact, freedom is found only by turning toward others, not by revolving around oneself in a downward narcissistic spiral. Don Giovanni never opens himself to the risk of a real relationship. Instead he counts his conquests. This calculating and acquisitive spirit is perfectly encapsulated in the opera's most celebrated aria of all, the "Catalogue Aria." Don Giovanni has just fled from confrontation with his jilted fiancée, Donna Elvira. He entrusts his manservant Leporello with the unenviable task of explaining things to her. Leporello gives her the full, unexpurgated list of his master's conquests: 640 Italian women, 231 German women, 100 in France, and in Turkey 91, but astonishing success in Spain, where 1,003 women have already yielded to his master's advances. The sum total comes to 2,065 women.

Part of the deceit of Don Giovanni is that both Donna Elvira and the audience believe he has seduced more than 2,000 women. Yet, no one seems to notice that in the opera itself, Don Giovanni is incapable of successfully seducing even one woman. Every time he tries to win someone over, he is thwarted. He is undoubtedly fixated on women, but he is also a total failure with them. Even though Leporello makes huge claims on his master's behalf, they are completely without foundation. Don Giovanni is all style and no substance. He reveals something about ourselves as well: something in us wants to believe the most ridiculous of lies; we prefer blown-up fantasies to the truth.

The character of Don Giovanni is a Babylonian figure, powerful and overtly seductive, sweeping us into his orbit by dint of sheer energy and passion. He sings so sweetly that his beguiling songs seem to be songs of love. Yet on closer inspection, they turn out to be vacuous and false. Their flickering glitter will never last long enough to truly glow. Don Giovanni comes across as a man full of life and adventure; but in reality, he limits himself to a thoroughly predictable and repetitive kind of conduct, the stale and repellent rhythm of conquest and disposal. He is a prisoner of lust, the most illusory of all capital sins because it is so enormously enticing, yet when surrendered to, is also spiritually fatal and emotionally deadening. Yet Mozart's music is so exquisite that it is almost humanly impossible not to identify at some level with the philandering protagonist whose life and energy dominate every moment of this astonishing opera.

The Irish writer James Joyce, another creative genius, was a pupil at Belvedere College, the Jesuit high school in Dublin where I had the privilege of spending two years as a rookie teacher. (When I began teaching there, a Jewish friend encouraged me to dream big dreams: "You'll be shaping future James Joyces," he promised me.) I read a third of Joyce's epic novel *Ulysses* before giving up. It is undoubtedly a work of genius, and also an excellent mirror of the stream of consciousness, but the stream that engages Joyce's attention is full of such vile flotsam and jetsam that much of it would have been better left unsaid. Whatever the literary critics may say, reading the story of a day in the life of Leopold Bloom did not give me wholesome desires or serenity, nor produce in me an increased closeness to God and others. I am inclined to agree with Roddy Doyle, a contemporary Irish writer, who found *Ulysses* much too long and claimed that Joyce would have benefited significantly from a sharp-eyed editor.

However, Joyce's short story "The Dead" touches me at a deep level. His imaginative genius transforms a painful memory from his own life into an uplifting work of fiction, a story of epiphany, a moment of insight and self-awareness, of genuine illumination. As he listens to his wife tell of the young boy Michael Furey, who died out of love for her, Gabriel Conroy begins to realize he has not been the only man in her life. He recognizes his littleness and unimportance in the grand scheme of things. He had deceived himself with illusions of his own greatness. He had placed himself at the center of things. Now he becomes vaguely conscious of something that has much vaster dimensions, something deep and unfathomable, and this elusive stirring of the imagination promises healing. He sees his own mortality, and also his connectedness with a world too mysterious to be named, let alone understood. As the snow falls at the close of the story, it allows Gabriel to forget the things that have kept him apart from others. In an exquisite final paragraph that is replete with repetition, alliteration, and the sheer musicality of language, a paragraph perhaps unequalled in the whole of English literature, the snow—"falling faintly through the universe and faintly falling"—descends upon each person, not just in Ireland, but everywhere. It is something from above that cleanses and unites as it spreads its peaceful, white, virgin mantle upon the landscape.

Our world needs the rejuvenation that beckons Gabriel Conroy at the close of this story. We need to rediscover passion as he is summoned to do. We need to be cleansed as the Irish landscape is in this story by something that is transcendent and that comes from beyond: something we cannot imagine, something or someone with the whiteness and purity of snow. We need to be challenged to move from shallowness to depth, from egoism to love, from isolation to connection, from self-absorption to respect for otherness, from drifting haphazardly to acquiring a specific direction. We need the amazing grace of a purified imagination.

The best advice I have found about purifying the imagination comes from the Letter to the Philippians 4:8. "Finally, beloved, whatever is true, whatever is honorable, whatever is just, whatever is pure, whatever is pleasing, whatever is commendable, if there is any excellence and if there is anything worthy of praise, think about these things." When Paul wrote these words to the Church at Philippi, he was a prisoner in Rome. Being under arrest at the time, he could easily have been troubled and anxious, consumed with self-pity or even anger. But Paul undoubtedly realized that filling his mind with bad things was more toxic to the spirit than bad food is damaging to the body. Whatever we feed grows even more, and whatever we starve dies. As Paul looked around during his imprisonment, he did not see many things to uplift him. So he had to use his imagination, and see things that were not there. He imagined things that were true, honorable, pure, right, excellent and worthy of praise. When the world around us looks dark and unforgiving, it is difficult not to be disheartened by the visible signs that drag us down. It demands a conscious effort and the help of grace not to succumb to disillusionment and bitterness. But the reward we reap more than worth it.

In the third chapter of the Letter to the Colossians (3:2), also dating from the time of Paul's imprisonment in Rome, there are once more some commanding words about the liberating power of an imagination that is upwardly focused: "Set your minds on things that are above, not on things that are on earth." Life is full of unpredictable events, ups and downs, twists and turns of fate that so easily and regularly throw us off balance. The imaginative key is not to be buffeted about by the stormy conditions, but to fix our eyes on God, to see that we are enfolded in divine love, to be certain that in all things—despite appearances—God is working for our good.

The imagination is an underrated element in our lives. It shapes us more than we realize, either through unhelpful images that lead us away from love, or else, if we consciously improve our mental seeing, with images that heal us into hope. The unredeemed imagination can sink us into trivialities or worse; the graced imagination can unveil new possibilities. The choice of which kind of imagination to follow is in our hands.

CHAPTER TEN
_____

Thinking Outside the Box

Logic will get you from A to B. Imagination will take you everywhere.

Albert Einstein

Visiting Shanghai, Sydney, Sao Paolo, or San Francisco, you may easily get a sinking feeling of sameness. You notice similar stores on the main streets of each of these cities. The people who walk past you there are wearing clothes with the same brand names, drinking the same types of cola. You look at the poster outside a movie theater: the film you saw last week in Los Angeles is also playing in Sydney. A car pulls up at the stoplight and you hear familiar hits blaring from the radio. It is understandable if you get the feeling that, after a fifteen-hour flight from California to Australia, you have not arrived in a different country at all but merely come back to your point of departure. Many of the world's big cities have become so alike that, in certain respects, they are indistinguishable. It is as if you hardly change cultures by moving from one big metropolis to another. Despite minor differences in inhabitants, architecture, and climate, these cities for the most part look the same.

Some people believe that a dominant global culture is dragging us all down to the lowest common dominator, a dumbed-down world dominated by frenetic celebrity gossip

and wacky snippets from YouTube. Others vehemently disagree: despite a few noticeable hiccups, they argue that the
world is progressing in a fundamentally positive direction.
But whatever about the basic direction, most sane people
would agree that we live in an imperfect world. There are all
sorts of reasons given for the imperfection of our world: war,
poverty, the debt of developing countries, trade protection-
ism, the credit crunch, al-Qaeda, tension in the Middle East,
globalization, nuclear weapons, disinformation on the Web,
unemployment, the collapse of the family, abortion, unemployment, consumerism, individualism, racism, sexism, funda-
mentalism, the overuse of natural resources, ozone depletion,
climate change….

There is no doubt that these are problems of great
magnitude. They deserve our attention and commitment,
and certainly we ought to take intelligent action when it
comes to these critical issues. But there is another major
malady that is for the most part overlooked, because we generally do not even realize it plays a part in our cultural
predicament. This *sickness* is staring us in the face. But we
do not see it because it is in front of our noses. There is
nothing technical or abstruse about it. It is a problem that
is thoroughly concrete. It is epitomized by the sensation
evoked above, the feeling that overcomes the international
traveler who encounters a standardized global culture in so
many big cities of the world with the same food, drink,
household appliances, pop songs, and fashions.

This sickness? The Western world view is *one-dimensional*.
We reduce the multifaceted reality of things to just one single
facet. For instance, culture can blind us to the truth that there
is more to education than examination results. Certainly
preparing for exams should not be neglected in education, but
deep down we all know that to flourish as individuals and

make a lasting contribution to the world, we need more than outstanding grade averages. Advertisements, movies, and the Internet proclaim that if you cannot have sex, you are unable to love. They tell people that sex is not just one expression of love, but that it is synonymous with the whole of love. The importance of a healthy sex life in marriage is not to be discounted, but love is bigger than sex. As the great Italian poet Dante Alighieri proclaimed at the end of his *Divine Comedy*, it is "love that moves the sun and other stars." Our culture shrinks communication to the transmission of information. The accurate transmission of information is vital to communication. But communication is much more than data transferal: it is a mutual exchange of meaning that enriches both partners in dialogue. If we focus exclusively on one dimension of education, work, or communication, we fail to see the depth and richness of each of these realities. We reduce each to a single feature. This is a recipe for blindness.

There is a story about a tribe of blind people who lived in a mountain village. One day they heard strange noises outside the wall that encircled their village. They presumed these noises came from a large animal of some kind. They sent a group of scouts to investigate. Had they been able to see, the scouts would have identified the mysterious animal immediately. But since they were blind, they could not have been expected to know that the animal in question was in fact an elephant. They approached the elephant and each scout touched a different part of it. When the scouts returned to the chief of the tribe, he asked each of them to report on what he had found. The scout who had touched the ear of the elephant said that the animal was about three foot long and four foot wide, thick and leafy, flapping like the wing of an eagle. But another scout who had stretched his hand along the elephant's trunk said it was like a periscope with a soft covering.

However, the scout who had touched one of the elephant's tusks disagreed: he said the animal was hard like limestone with a sharp point at one end. The scout who had touched one of the elephant's legs offered a completely different perspective, insisting that the animal was a solid straight pillar.

Each scout touched one part of the elephant, and each confused this one part with the whole of the elephant. What each scout said was true, but it was only a partial truth. In the same way, if we pay attention to only one aspect of culture, we end up with only a truncated version of the truth: we blind ourselves to the richness and diversity of reality. Each of the scouts distinguished different parts of the elephant. We need to distinguish different aspects of cultural reality. But distinguishing them is not enough. We also have to come to understand how the different parts fit together into a totality. This totality does not abolish the differences, just like the integral wholeness of the elephant does not eliminate the different features—ears, tusks, legs, trunk, and so on—that make it up. In fact, it is because these parts fit together into a coherent and living whole that we have this marvelous animal we call an elephant. In order to get the bigger picture, we need to see how things like family, work, and education have many layers of meaning, and how each is simultaneously connected with other dimensions of life. If we limit ourselves to a single narrow meaning of something like work, we end up blinding ourselves to other more liberating aspects of it. We narrow our goals to making as much money as we can, without asking how we can contribute to the well-being of society. We thus miss out on confronting wider questions or adopting new courses of action.

With the help of a multilayered view, we think outside the box, and we see things from fresh angles. A multifaceted perspective welcomes alternative ways of seeing, thinking, and acting. It opens up to and befriends the possible. This deeper view is necessary in order to envisage the environment, our health, the sexes, and so many other aspects of our lives together in a fuller and richer way. We suffer from cultural malnutrition when we get ambushed by one meaning of a particular word. For example, certain Asian cultures are predisposed to view the term *authority* as a good thing, which inclines them to overlook abuses of power, or the ways in which authority can be used to coerce and manipulate people. Some Western cultures are immediately suspicious of the term *authority*, finding it difficult to believe that authority can be a form of service for the good of everyone.

It takes inventiveness to view different facets of a single reality and discern a connection. It is like putting two things side by side that seemingly do not belong together. When it comes to ourselves, we deny our greatness by viewing ourselves from merely one angle. Self-descriptions are limiting when they confine us to one level of our humanity. There are people who say to themselves, "I am a worm," and never realize that there is also a butterfly inside them. This lack of imagination is understandable. If you were to look at a plain green caterpillar next to a yellow and black Tiger Swallowtail butterfly, you might find it difficult to imagine that the destiny of this ugly and snake-like caterpillar is to become that beautiful and fragile butterfly. The butterfly is not a big worm or a large-size caterpillar: it is something qualitatively different. The caterpillar does not simply change in order to turn into a butterfly: it is transformed. Many people fail to realize that their lives could be transformed; the mere idea smacks too much of fairy-tales and Hollywood movies. They cannot seriously entertain the idea.

How can we think outside the box when it comes to life, liberty, and the pursuit of happiness? For it is the value we place upon these three essentials that truly decides who we are. Happiness is what everyone wants, the ultimate goal in life. There are many different conceptions of happiness. Consumerist society offers us a vision of happiness that is inextricably linked to possessions and power, to rank and reputation. There must be a grain of truth in this vision of happiness; otherwise, it would not be so compelling. We all want money. But on reflection, we do not want money so much for its own sake as for its effects: the prestige, power, and recognition it brings in its wake. Because money is not the highest goal, but only sought to give us something higher, money itself is not happiness. What about the more desirable objectives that money helps us attain—power, status, reputation: are they what happiness entails? We all like to be recognized, and being admired for our achievements is especially gratifying. However, this kind of happiness is an "outside thing": it depends on what others think of us, and if others change their high opinion of us, they take away our happiness. If happiness is the highest goal in life, it should be solid enough to withstand the sudden shifts in people's esteem of us, even though these will inevitably have some effect on our happiness, since none of us lives alone or is happy alone. Yet despite the fact that external factors and even chance contribute to happiness, it is predominantly an inside thing, something that has deeper roots than fame or reputation. In fact, perhaps happiness is not a thing that we can ever conquer once and for all, but only pursue.

The U.S. Declaration of Independence wisely refers to our right to *pursue* happiness. To live happily does not mean to *possess* the perfect spouse, the ideal career, a high income, and universal adulation. To live happily is not about the destination but the journey. It is about being on a journey where all our forward progress expresses what is deepest in ourselves, and therefore brings us real and lasting joy. To live happily is to direct ourselves toward a goal that surpasses us, and to consecrate our talents and resources to that uplifting goal. We need to find out what activity in life energizes us most, makes us feel most ourselves, most alive, and gives us most joy. This is where we pursue our happiness. And although we are not obliged to dismiss other activities in our life, they must give precedence to this one ruling activity.

How do we live freely? Just as there are levels of happiness, there are levels of freedom. The most basic level of freedom is freedom from restrictions. It is the freedom of someone who is released from prison, or of a worker relieved of the pressure of cares and responsibilities. It is the freedom to follow our natural inclinations without outside interference. A second and higher level of freedom is the freedom to choose. In Western culture, the individuals with the widest range of choices appear to be the freest of all. Individuals with money, power, fame, and connections epitomize freedom in our eyes, because these qualities enable them to do things that many others are simply unable to do. They walk into an exclusive restaurant and a table is ready for them; they pick up a phone and things happen; people line up to do their bidding. There is a shadow side to such enormous freedom as well: the fear that all one's money could be lost, that one's reputation could be torn to shreds, that one's fame could degenerate into notoriety.

Freedom of choice is a great blessing when we use it to choose goodness. But freedom of choice does not bring us far if we only seek it for its own sake—what is the point of being able to choose from a hundred brands of perfumes or clothes if you cannot choose to be yourself? Freedom of choice is at its best when it serves self-realization. We are not free simply for the heck of it, but in order to become all we can be as human beings. We have to use freedom carefully, because although we are free to make big decisions, once we do we are stuck with the consequences. We are free to shoot a gun, but once we pull the trigger we have no more control over the trajectory of the bullets. We are free to choose, but we are not free when it comes to the consequences of our choices. It is analogous to the "butterfly effect," the idea that an apparently insignificant event like the flapping of a tiny butterfly's wings in Hong Kong can trigger a complex chain of natural events that eventually leads to a devastating tornado in Texas. Our choices may seem inconsequential when we make them, but in retrospect they can alter entire destinies: if, for example, the man who was to become your father had not been there to pick up the glove a young woman dropped on Fifth Avenue in January 1959, he would never have proposed to her, and you would not exist today.

Freedom is not absolutely free, but has a certain inbuilt price of "should." Freedom is not merely doing what I want, but becoming the person I ought to become. It is not about following my instincts, but about committing myself to a person (as your father did), a cause, or an ideal. Freedom presupposes that the purpose of human nature is not simply to remain as it is, but to become more than it is. Freedom is about going beyond the limitations of who we are now to become fuller human beings. Our destiny as human beings is to go beyond our nature, to break through limits, and to give a distinctive and unique seal to our identity.

Every society aims for some version of the good life. Vietnam is dominated by the Taoist vision of life, which insists on the importance of being in harmony with nature in order to find happiness. The Tao represents the natural order of things, encapsulated by sayings such as, "When spring comes, the grass grows by itself." Nature is generally considered differently in the West, where it is essentially regarded as something to be managed and controlled, not something to be submitted to as a given. Thus everything and anything seem possible, since we can become who we want to be and not what nature decides for us. No society perfectly hits the target of goodness: the Taoist approach to life can be reproached for its sense of fatalism and resignation; the Western attitude for its unwillingness to accept the limitations of nature and destiny. But whatever the imperfections of particular societies, we all seek the good in some way or another. And all of us like good things, because they develop and enrich us. Goodness always urges us to choose it, because it is radiant and attractive. It is a magnet that draws us toward the fullness of being human.

Because no society is perfect, it would be wonderful to draw out the best from each nation and unite them all into a winning tapestry. Someone light-heartedly suggested that in a perfect world the lovers would be Italian, the cooks French, the hoteliers Swiss, the mechanics German, and the police officers English. However, if we got things wrong and made the lovers Swiss, the cooks English, the hoteliers Italian, the mechanics French, and the police officers German, we could be in for a hellish time!

We are the most exasperating and exciting of all creatures on this tiny planet of ours, a fascinating and frustrating mixture of wonderful generosity and absurd pettiness. We are ready to change the whole world for the better until a mosquito sting completely derails us from our lofty aspirations. It is heartening that, despite our contradictions, so many of us hunger for real life, full liberty, and the right to pursue happiness.

In the final chapter of his monumental book *The Critique of Pure Reason*, the German philosopher Immanuel

Kant gives a wonderfully concise overview of philosophy. According to Kant, philosophy pursues three fundamental questions: What can I know? What ought I do? What may I hope for? These three questions in turn boil down to a fourth question that embraces them all: What is the human being? Every generation and every society has to ask these questions over and over again.

What can we know about society? We can know so many different aspects of society: the way people speak, how they rear families, how they make peace and war....We know that culture is made up of light and shade, and that life is too big a burden for too many people. But we also know the truth of what our world can be, and if we put this truth into practice, it will steadily set us free and bring us happiness.

What ought we do when it comes to society? Remembering that, in the final analysis, society is our creation and exists for our sake, we ought to make society more human, an incubator and nurturer of human freedom. Every society communicates a value system; it is crucial to ensure that this system of values builds up human beings instead of tearing them down. We ought not to accept everything around us in a naïve and unthinking way. But neither should we dismiss our world as unredeemable. We ought to be open to our social world in a compassionate yet discerning way. We must be alert to the direction it takes and ask, where is it leading us? Every avalanche starts with a snowflake; it is possible to intervene when only a few snowflakes have accumulated, but once the avalanche is hurtling toward us, there is little we can do. We ought to ensure that our society is leading us toward life and not death, in the direction of freedom and not imprisonment, to the pursuit of happiness and not to less-worthy quests.

What may we hope for from society? We have no right to hope for everything from society, because it cannot satisfy

139

all our yearnings. It is not paradise on earth. But we can dare hope that it will be as close to perfection as possible by guaranteeing us life, liberty, and the pursuit of happiness. We may dare hope that love will win out over hatred, that goodness will triumph over evil, that trust will quench our lingering suspicions and doubts. We have not yet arrived at the kind of world we want. But we are working on improving it. The hope of a better West lies ahead, just beyond our line of vision, but visible to the eyes of our imagination. Let us dare to imagine with boldness.

CHAPTER ELEVEN

Beyond Babylon

All men dream, but not equally. Those who dream by
night in the dusty recesses of their minds wake in
the day to find that it was vanity: but the dreamers
of the day are dangerous men, for they may act on
their dreams with open eyes, to make them possible.

T. E. Lawrence

Ever since Adam blamed Eve and Eve in turn blamed the ser-
pent, we human beings have displayed an incredible capacity
to disclaim responsibility and point the finger at others. The
identity of the infamous Babylon the Great in the Apocalypse
or the Book of Revelation is a case in point. This final book of
the Bible is full of exaggerated and unrestrained images and
symbols. Although it is one of the most enigmatic books of the
Bible, this much is clear: it was written to give hope to Christians in a time of huge difficulties, and to reassure them that
despite all the evidence to the contrary, goodness would eventually triumph. Probably the best-known metaphor in the
whole book is that of the harlot Babylon, which is certainly not
intended to be taken literally. It stands for those who collude
in doing what is wrong.

The last thing most Christians would want to admit is
that they themselves may be part of this ghastly Babylon, that
they themselves could be serious or serial wrongdoers. They

are more than willing to countenance that it could be anyone else: from pagan Rome to contemporary consumerist society to other Christian denominations.

But what if this "whore" of Babylon *is* us—not just Christians, but all of us, all human beings on the face of the earth? After all, the Book of Revelation has a cosmic perspective. It is looking at things in terms of the whole universe, and you do not have to be a UFO fanatic to suspect that out there among the hundreds of billions of stars in galaxy upon galaxy, there must be a large number of terrestrial planets like our own, some of which are habitable and inhabited.

God is not lazy and is certainly not short on ideas or resources. I cannot imagine God being satisfied creating just a single race, our human one, especially given how terribly inhuman our track record has been over the centuries. God is infinite love: if I were even remotely similar, I would be more than keen to share my abundance with as many creatures as possible. If I were a Creator, I would delight in generating world upon world. It is terribly patronizing on our part to reduce God to the shrunken dimensions of our own imaginations, and to suppose that all he can create— apart from us, the angels, and life on earth—is a dumb and inanimate universe. How insulting is that!

I already blush at the thought of the Day of Judgment, not so much at the prospect of standing next to so many of my fallible fellow human beings from this planet, but at the shameful probability that I will undoubtedly want to sink into a bottomless black hole when I see the turbo-charged goodness of billions upon billions of beings from other planets. Not only do I believe there are other inhabited worlds in our universe; I also have a strong hunch that they have lived better lives than we human beings as a whole have managed to do. When I see these better beings at the end of time, I am sure I will feel like a pauper next to a plethora of princes, a beast confronted with unimaginable beauty, a Neolithic man lost in Manhattan. There may be seven wonders in this world, but God has fashioned innumerable breathtaking worlds elsewhere.

This future scenario in my imagination gives me a clue about how to get beyond Babylon in my real life today. If I am going to find myself confronted by such amazing beings, and indeed by the most astonishing Being of all—God, then that future vision of Truth will inevitably force me to become humble, to recognize how small and insufficient I am by comparison. However, instead of waiting for humility to be forced upon me in the next life, it makes sense to start cultivating it in this one.

It takes humility to admit that we are Babylon. It takes humility to confess that we will never stop being Babylon if we try to get out of Babylon by ourselves. The only way to escape this corrupt metropolis is by accepting the help of Someone who can take us by the hand and lead us out. Being humble means acknowledging we cannot make it on our own, but simultaneously believing that everything is possible with God.

Before I start extolling humility, I must face the fact that humility has bad press. It conjures up images of self-disgust and abject groveling, of people without any backbone at all. Frankly, such a spineless anthropology makes any right-minded person squirm. How can adults who have come of age even contemplate returning to the infantile dependence of humility? How can anyone be misguided enough to see humility as progress when it seems to drag us downward?

These questions need to be taken seriously, and they point to the fact that we can only take our humble status seriously on condition that we also hold our greatness before our eyes. We may be clay creatures, but we are also immortal diamonds. We must admit all that we are not, while at the same time seeing all that we are.

Although we are right to be suspicious of a humility that is disingenuous and descends into self-hatred, we must also be honest enough to admit that our Western culture has gone to the other extreme, puffing up pride and being too harsh on humility. It espouses independence over interdependence, it promotes the winners instead of the ones who serve, and it prefers self-glorification to self-knowledge.

Humility is truthfulness and means accepting the truth: we are human beings, and not God. A humble person is mercifully free of illusions. Often we are tempted to put ourselves above the truth, and pretend we are what we are not: God. The most difficult idol to demolish is the idol that speaks in the first person, and makes a god of me. But the truth is that I am not the center of the universe, and neither is the planet upon which I live. It is not about making "my kingdom come" or saying, "my will be done." Since I am not the center of the world, I should not be totally preoccupied with myself: I should leave room for others. More than that, I should be radically open to others. If I want to get out of Babylon, I should give myself over to the risky adventure of love.

There is a stirring story about humility in chapter 5 of Luke's Gospel. Jesus is about to call Peter to follow him. But first he decides to teach him a thing or two about something that Peter thinks he knows inside out: fishing. Jesus gets into a boat with Peter and his companions. Peter respects Jesus as a distinguished Rabbi, but when it comes to fishing, Peter feels the master. It is not surprising, given his long years on the Lake of Gennesaret. So he is taken aback when Jesus suggests throwing his nets in exactly the same spot where he has just been fishing all night without success. Peter cannot refrain from hinting that this is a bad idea, but out of indulgence for this kind but misguided Rabbi, he reluctantly agrees to cast the nets in that spot. Seconds later, he makes the biggest catch of his life: there are so many fish flapping and writhing inside the nets that they begin to strain and tear with the weight. Peter gets the help of neighboring fishermen to haul this stupendous catch ashore.

It is only then that the shock of it all hits Peter. He is full of wonder at the huge catch, but feels even greater wonder at being before the one who made that catch possible. Just like the contrast of the empty nets the night before and the full catch just now, Peter also keenly feels his own emptiness before the fullness of Jesus. He kneels down before Jesus and asks him to leave. "I am a sinful man," he explains (Luke 5:8). Peter has encountered a dimension that is beyond him. He feels totally inadequate. All he sees is his own fragile humanity. But seeing emptiness on its own is not the fullness of humility. Jesus promises Peter that his fragility and emptiness in fact conceal a great power, full of presence. Genuine humility has astonishing force. It may seem like nothing, but it is all. Jesus promises Peter that he will make an unprecedented catch in a completely different realm, as he invites this bewildered man to dare "fish" for human beings. Peter's nothingness will combine with God's greatness to form a potent and irresistible mix. His apparent descent into weakness is in fact a rising into strength. He will end up accomplishing astonishing things. He will transform himself and others in improbable and happy ways.

What does it mean to be humble? Three things: realizing I need God and others, honestly acknowledging my gifts and limitations, and casting the "net" of my life into the ocean of loving service.

First, the Bible never tires of highlighting the importance of realizing our dependence upon God. The very origins of the nation of Israel are to be found in the most oppressed ethnic group in Egypt, which is liberated from slavery by God and guided to the Promised Land. The memory of this dependence is evident in prayer after prayer, as the Jewish people recall their indebtedness to God. The Bible suggests that only God could be the source of their startling ability to survive despite all the opposition and hostility they encounter. The Virgin Mary echoes the cry of gratitude that constantly crossed the lips of her ancestors: "The Mighty One has done great things for me" (Luke 1:49). In our own lives, we realize that none of us can become ourselves without others. The Irish poet and playwright Aidan Mathews gives eloquent expression to our dependence upon others:

> Whether in a state of conflict or community, whether popular or polarised, we are plural creatures before we are singular creations, we are social before we are solitary. We are born from others and we will be buried by others; and in between, others, whether as role models or rivals, as mentors or tormentors (and usually as both at the same time), will be the gauntlet and the honour guard of our being in the world.[1]

Accurate self-knowledge is the second indispensable aspect of humility. The Bible emphasizes two vital features of who we are. The first thing it tells us—both chronologically and in order of importance—is that we are created in the image and likeness of God. We are of inestimable value in God's eyes, truly precious. In fact, the Creator has made us little less than gods, crowning us with glory and honor.

The Bible also makes clear that at the same time we are fallen and fallible creatures. But it is important to remember that by nature we are great; the fallen part came later. We are *essentially* great, and we should never forget this. What makes us great is the divine spark within us. This spark is the soul. It is a spark that is kindled by God. When we begin to marvel at life, our soul is joyously exploring the wonder of existence. When we love not by instinct but with free will, our soul is at work. When we become beautiful inside, our soul reveals itself. The soul is a living gem that glows brightly when we live good lives, but loses its luster when we do wrong.

The third crucial characteristic of humble persons is that they reach out in service. They do not cling to titles or status. They are willing to empty themselves in order to serve others. They do not lord it over others, but appeal to them through the goodness of their lives.

We will never get out of Babylon unless we do it together. Humble people reach out because they feel responsible for others, but not in a coldly dutiful way. This liberating responsibility is illustrated by a breathtaking story in Dostoevsky's *The Brothers Karamazov*. We discover that an elderly monk named Zosima, who plays a key role in the novel, has learned a deep lesson from his dying brother Markel. As he is succumbing to a deathly illness, Markel utters these puzzling words: "Every one of us has sinned against all men, and I more than any."[2] What can Markel possibly mean? How can he live with such words that seem to impose a crushing weight of guilt and obligation? Surprisingly, Markel's deep conviction of his own responsibility is also the source of his extraordinary happiness, of a deep sense of consolation that makes his suffering bearably light. This truth is so clear to him that he repeats it even more forcefully: "Believe me, everyone is really responsible to all men for all men and for everything."[3] As his strength ebbs away, Markel feels intensely grateful, and it is almost as though his heart expands in love to embrace all of creation. His poor mother is puzzled by Markel's utterances, and the doctor who is treating him takes these outbursts as conclusive evidence that the disease is affecting his brain. But after Markel dies, his new credo changes the life of his brother Zosima, who has previously been a carefree and self-absorbed young man.

When Zosima slights a wealthy landowner in public, the two decide to resolve matters through a duel. The evening before, Zosima vents his anger upon his hapless servant, beating him until the poor man's face is covered in blood. When he awakes the next morning, the images of the evening before come back to haunt him. Zosima breaks down crying and the words of his dead brother Markel return to him: "In truth, perhaps, I am more than all responsible for all, a greater sinner than all men in the world."[4] Zosima reflects that he is prepared to kill a man who has never done him any wrong, but whom *he* has publicly insulted. He is ready to rob this man of his life. In a fit of remorse, Zosima gets down on his knees before his servant, bending his forehead to the ground, and begs for forgiveness. His servant is thoroughly perplexed by this abrupt change in his master's conduct. Zosima hastens to the site of the duel, allows the landowner to take the first shot, after which Zosima promptly throws his loaded pistol to the ground, begging his antagonist to forgive him, explaining that he is ten times worse a person than the landowner could ever possibly be.

Some of Zosima's friends are amused by his religious turn; others mock him outright. A stranger starts visiting Zosima, and encourages him on this new path. The man tells Zosima that although he might appear to be a simpleton, he is in fact doing something that could transform the world, if only everyone acted likewise: "And in very truth, so soon as men understand that, the Kingdom of Heaven will be for them not a dream, but a living reality."[5]

Usually the words *responsibility* and *sinner* turn us off. But in the case of Markel, and later his brother Zosima, these words and the realities they represent are liberating. The reason is because it is not a responsibility either of them has to carry alone. They have both responded to the gravitational pull of God, and so their yoke is easy and their burden is light. Love has given them wings. They have renounced their attempts to run their own lives, and in surrendering themselves to God, they experience a joy that lifts them. They have become so attuned to God that they have also gracefully tuned into the wavelength of service.

Truly humble people share the deep compassion of Zosima. They may be saddened when others are unresponsive, but they do not lose their serenity through making harsh judgments. Instead, they step into the shoes of ungrateful people, trying to love in their place. They plead with God to shine forth his love upon bad as well as good, upon the indifferent as well as the committed. They do not rely upon their own resources, and their trust in God is so overwhelming that God cannot but respond to their prayers. They are kind enough to see that the badness of most people is due to the little love they have received in their lives. They give their hearts and heads and hands to God so that God may work through them.

As well as humility, we need hope, the confidence to trust that God can free us from all our bad places and spaces, from all our Babylons. God knows we have our worries. With the new fragility of the world economy, we in the Western world are painfully walking through uncharted territory. With the erosion of financial security, our personal freedom to pursue what society offers has been seriously undermined. Everything is affected by crippling economic uncertainty: we cannot afford the best education for our children; the promise of secure jobs has become a mirage; we are unable to benefit from good health care; and a worry-free retirement is now a pipedream. We can no longer live where we want, or take care of our families as we would like. In fact, family relationships are under severe strain because of our economic difficulties. Some parts of the world are in constant turmoil. Even in the relative security of the West, we sit in our apartments and hope more hijacked planes will not fly into us. We take the subway and cannot quite dismiss the fear that we may become victims of a random bomb or gas attack. Strangely, the threat that seems most distant is that for which the evidence is relentlessly mounting: global warming. We hear constant reports of melting glaciers and sea ice, warming oceans, increasing levels of carbon dioxide in the atmosphere, and spreading tropical diseases, but it just does not sound like something that will really affect most of us in our own backyards.

Our topsy-turvy period of history is encapsulated well by the opening lines of Charles Dickens' *A Tale of Two Cities*:

> It was the best of times, it was the worst of times, it was the age of wisdom, it was the age of foolishness, it was the epoch of belief, it was the epoch of incredulity, it was the season of Light, it was the season of Darkness, it was the spring of hope, it was the winter of despair, we had everything before us, we had nothing before us, we were all going direct to Heaven, we were all going direct the other way.[6]

When we are in the midst of darkness, the light seems a world away. We become stuck and lose confidence. We wonder if we shall ever emerge from despair. We need wisdom in this time of upheaval—not book knowledge, but knowledge that can change our lives and help us make the right ethical choices.

The worst thing we can do is to despair. Where there is life, there is always hope; and hope should never be postponed. When we hope, we refuse to be imprisoned in the difficult circumstances of the present moment; instead, we reach forward to a better future, overcoming our fear that the future might be just a sad extension of the troubles of today. In dark times above all, our hope needs to be founded on something of infinite power: God.

We need to cultivate the collective human spirit anew. We need to learn how to live well again, which includes physical, psychological, economic, and spiritual well-being. We need to cultivate our bodies to become healthy, our emotional lives to become mature, and our way of making a living to become profitable. But being physically perfect, psychologically well-adjusted, and economically successful, while all desirable, do not exhaust the meaning of life. We also need to cultivate our imaginations. The literary critic Denis Donoghue eulogizes the mysterious power of the imagination:

> Let us say then, that the imagination is the secular name we apply to the soul when we wish to live peacefully with our neighbours. I cannot believe that the imagination is other than divine in its origin; but even if we leave that belief aside, or disagree upon it, we may agree that the imagination is a form of energy, demonstrable in its consequences if not in its nature, and that it strives to

> realise itself by living in the world. Like the soul,
> the imagination seeks to inhabit not only a human
> body but a human world.[7]

Hope propels us toward great things, and it is the imagination that gives us the entrance ticket into the hope-filled world of possibility. In these uncertain times, we must strive against the odds to give ourselves the freedom that comes from standing on the threshold of possibility. In the midst of an impossible situation in India, Mahatma Gandhi had the imagination to employ nonviolent tactics. After all, what is more creative than defeating a ruler without engaging in war? When the imagination gets to work, it can be marvelously inventive. The imagination should not be dismissed as mere fancy, for it achieves its fruitful results not only through inspiration, but also through the perspiration of disciplined effort and sacrifice. It is not just idle dreaming, but something profoundly ethical, offering a vision of a new kind of cultural life.

There is no denying the destructive impact economically hard times have upon us, not to mention the deliberate violence of terrorists and the thousand natural shocks that the flesh is heir to. Yet ultimately it is not external enemies from which we most need to be saved; it is from our miserly imaginations and cheapened ideals, our easily satisfied notions of life. We are beings who can be much more than we think. Hope pushes us toward our best possibilities. There is still time to reach toward being the person you always wanted to be.

The world in which we live is neither Armageddon nor Nirvana; it embraces both negative and positive. How can we live with reality in all its messiness? We must come to understand the complexity of our world better, learn how to cope with its shadow sides, and get the best we can from its more positive features.

Our world is undoubtedly complex. A line from Wallace Stevens' long poem "The Auroras of Autumn" (1948) sums up the reassuring security of the nostalgic world of yesterday: "We were as Danes in Denmark all day long." For many of us, the world of the past appears simpler, a world in which our ancestors had a relatively straightforward and nonproblematic relationship with others. No doubt we look back with rose-colored glasses. It is tempting to idealize what has gone before as some halcyon sphere. But it was also a time of small horizons that lacked excitement and diversity. Nevertheless, it provided roots that allowed room for growth. It was a pre-dominantly rural world, where people had deep anchors in the small and complete cultures of villages and towns. In our own millennium, on May 23, 2007, to be exact, a seismic and relatively unnoticed shift in the world's population came to pass: for the first time in human history, the number of human beings living in cities exceeded those living in rural areas. The rural world of yesterday was a more settled and static world, where people felt like fish in water, even if the pond at times was claustrophobic. Now the rural world has given way to the urban sprawl.

Today we are aware that there are so many different worlds: someone who visits China realizes that this bewildering language that sounds so strange is in fact natural for the more than one billion inhabitants who make up the most populous nation on earth. Before the exponential rise in international travel and the arrival of the information superhighway, even tiny provincial cultures appeared natural because they were all that many people knew. "We were as Danes in Denmark all day long." Who speaks Danish today? Five million people in Scandinavia, a tiny drop in the ocean of humanity. Danish is one of more than 7,000 languages spoken on our planet.

In this world of dizzying complexity, we fear that "something is rotten in the state of Denmark" (*Hamlet*, 1.iv) and indeed throughout Western culture. If a banking crisis in Iceland has a domino effect on London's Oxford Street and a thousand other places, how can we pull ourselves back together again? After all, if Humpty Dumpty falls from the wall today, a lot of people fall with him, and many other walls come tumbling down as well. We used to imagine that, despite the diversity within particular societies and across the world, we could somehow all aspire to safe middle-class ambitions like basic financial security, a wholesome family life, an education for excellence, a fulfilling job with a handsome wage, good health and white teeth, a house in the suburbs, freedom to worship, protection from terrorism, and an environment ready to do our bidding. Now life is no longer so straightforward.

We are not here only to make money, though we need that too. We are not here just to enjoy good health, though we all know what an incredible difference that makes. We are not here solely to live morally good lives, admirable though upright living is. We are here for a project so audacious that something within us finds it hard to believe: we are here to transform ourselves and our world. If we cannot believe this, it is because we have downsized our beliefs. It is our greatness rather than our littleness that intimidates us most of all. But hope can heal us, for hope unsettles us with the passionate unrest that aims for the greatest things possible.

The controversial German philosopher Martin Heidegger gave a famous interview to the German magazine *Der Spiegel* in May 1976. The interview had the title, "Only a God Can Save Us." As a young philosopher, Heidegger himself had thought for a while that the rise of Nazism was the godlike event that would liberate Germans and all of humanity. Despite his sinister kinship with National Socialism, there is a rich suggestiveness in Heidegger's phrase that "only a god can save us," and it can be interpreted independently of the seductive evil of Nazism. It suggests that we cannot get out of this morass by dint of sheer willpower, that we cannot lift ourselves up by our own bootstraps. The economy won't save us, and technology and science are both incapable of redeeming us. We need to be saved by Someone from beyond, Someone not subject to our control and not at the mercy of our caprice. In dark times, the light is not visible, yet it can be sensed. Heidegger's favorite poet Hölderlin tellingly proclaimed, "But where danger is / grows the saving power also."[8]

Some people have forgotten God, and this is the greatest tragedy of our time: for when we forget God, we also forget ourselves and what it means to be human. Even those who remember God are not so sure they can rely upon the All-Holy One. They have recreated God in their own image, and find it difficult to believe that God is trustworthy, that God is beyond anything they can ask for or imagine. But for all that, God is still a God in whom we can hope, for God is the true fulfillment of everything for which we long and desire. God promises us that the best is yet to come.

Hope encourages us to believe in our own highest possibilities. Humility teaches us not to be totally unrealistic about these possibilities. Hope invites us to choose whatever makes us grow most. Hope lends our hearts a holy restlessness that is never satisfied with the status quo. Humility reminds us that we are nevertheless creatures, and not gods. Difficulty does not destroy hope, though it does make holding onto it more precarious. In fact, when the cultural situation becomes critical, and everything turns against us, we are willing to try remedies that we would never entertain in our saner moments. It is precisely at moments such as these that we are open to transforming our life, because we are prepared to court the big risks it entails. The risk is worth it, because without risk we can lose out on life altogether. Transformation is not a matter of tinkering with one or two things; it is radical change. It is moving from cozy comfort to hazardous happiness. At the same time, humility tempers our exuberance by keeping us grounded in a sense of who we truly are.

The challenging news is that our way of life must change. The good news is that our way of life *can* change: we are at a learnable moment. Our difficult global situation gives us the incentive to make radical changes. We are coming to the end of an era, and we must be brave enough to relinquish a vision of life, even though this leaves us fearful and uncertain because we are abandoning a part of who we are.

Ultimately our vision of life needs to be expanded in all directions—heightened, broadened, and deepened. Our vision of happiness is too petty and parsimonious. We want to be happy but in limited ways: we are reluctant to lose our economic privileges, downgrade our jobs, or accept sacrifices as the inevitable price of a better existence for all. We prefer a comfortable happiness centered on ourselves, where others sooner or later become the means to our own fulfillment. We are invited instead into a larger kind of happiness, which we cannot own, but only pursue. Nature does not deliver us as finished products. Through the way we live, we must complete the process of becoming human beings, a process that is never finished. And it is through relinquishing a life focused on the ego that we become truly alive.

Our vision of liberty must be transformed. We have inherited a limited view from our parents, from our educa-

tion, and from our society. We need to deepen it. True freedom is the freedom to love, a small word but a huge reality,
because only love is without limits. Love makes extraordinary demands. It is radical and insistent, a freedom so deep
you cannot see the bottom of its ocean, a freedom so high it
is dizzying.

Although the imagination in the form of useless fan-
tasy can distract us from what is truly important, at its best
the imagination can show us things as they can be, and not
as they are. Through the graced imagination, God helps us
see the world in a new way. The graced imagination has
three forms, corresponding to the three tenses of our lives:
past, present, and future. Let's call these three temporal
expressions of the redeemed imagination the *Emmaus* imagination, the *Evangelical* imagination, and the *Easter* imagination.

The *Emmaus* imagination teaches us to reinterpret the
past in a positive light, to see rumors of angels where once
we saw only cause for fear and worry. At times we are so
overcome by anxiety that we fail to connect the dots that
give a narrative thread of hope to our lives. Finding hope
does not mean ignoring the hurts or whitewashing the past.
Tellingly, in the story of the road to Emmaus from the
Gospel of Luke, the two disciples must first share their own
disappointment and unburden themselves, before they are
ready to hear the more liberating account of past events
from the mouth of the still-unrecognized Jesus who is walking beside them. It is only after God and others have
patiently listened to our inner struggles and pains that we
are open to seeing experience with the healed eyes of hope.
The Emmaus imagination is not an instantaneous acquisi-
tion: we must go through a process before we are graced
with a new take on our experience, a perspective that comes

above all from listening to the Word of God and breaking bread together.

The *Evangelical* imagination teaches us to live the present moment in a new way by seeing the "good news" that God is in our neighbor. Thanks to the Evangelical imagination we can reimagine the people around us here and now as images of God. To love God is also to love simultaneously everything that resembles God, everything that reminds us of God, everything that God loves. Most of all, it is to love our neighbor. If we believe that God is in our neighbor and in the events of our lives, we can live our love creatively by finding God everywhere. But if we do not seek the link between love for the God whom we cannot see, and love for our brothers and sisters whom we can see, our love will be weakened and destroyed. If we give people lukewarm love, we offer nothing but tasteless charity to God. If we are not fully present to them, we are also somewhat absent from God. If we do not serve them, we render God a disservice. At the end of each day, we can measure our Evangelical imagination, and find out how much we really loved God today by thinking back to the person we loved least during the course of the day.

The *Easter* imagination teaches us to face the future with the certainty that all will be transformed, that beyond all death is sheer life. Precisely because of its unknown quality, the death that ends this life is a test of our trust and our love. It offers us the opportunity to show God the biggest proof of love and the ultimate act of trust, by believing that beyond death is not darkness but light, not silence but the merciful voice of God, who will speak more loving words to us than we have ever managed to hear on earth. The Easter imagination calls us to lay aside our fear of death, and rehearse already the celebrations that will mark the birthday of our new life. God dares us to die for love of him as Jesus died for love of us.

Summing up: a renewed imagination helps us see and seize new possibilities in our past, present, and future. It enables us to experience the world in a fresh way, understand it differently, and respond to it creatively. We can grit our teeth all we like, and exercise our will power to the utmost, but without the graced imagination, our souls shall never catch fire. The redeemed imagination presents us with images of how we can live and who we can be, images that attract our will and galvanize us into action. Our summons is to imagine—and firmly believe—we can become all that God wants us to be, by taking up the divine invitation to live beyond ourselves, for God and for others.

Notes

Chapter 1

1. http://www.ad2000.com.au/articles/2000/may2000 p13_58.html. Accessed on December 14, 2011.

2. http://www.mfa.gov.il/MFA/Government/Speeches+ by+Israeli+leaders/2000/Visit+of+Pope+John+Paul+II- +Address+by+PM+Barak+at.htm?DisplayMode=print. Accessed on December 14, 2011.

Chapter 2

1. Black-Eyed Peas, "Where Is the Love?" Music and lyrics by William James Adams, Jr. (stage name: will.i.am); Jaime Luis Gómez (stage name: Taboo); Allan Pineda Lindo, Jr. (stage name: apl.de.ap); Ron Fair; Printz Board; George Pajon, Jr.; Michael Fratantuno; J. Curtis; and Justin Timberlake. From *Elephunk*, A&M Records, 2003.

Chapter 3

1. Charles Dickens, *Hard Times*, edited with an intro- duction by Paul Schlicke (Oxford: Oxford University Press, 2008), 6.

2. *Être et Avoir* ("To Be and To Have"), directed by Nicolas Philibert, 2002, produced by Maïa Films. Translation from the French by the author.

Chapter 5

1. Karl Marx, *Capital: An Abridged Edition*, edited with an introduction by David McLellan (Oxford University Press, 1999), 116.

Chapter 6

1. Hans Jonas, *The Imperative of Responsibility: In Search of an Ethics for the Technological Age*, translated by Hans Jonas with the collaboration of David Herr (Chicago: The University of Chicago Press, 1984).

2. Ibid., 11.

3. Douglas Coupland, *Girlfriend in a Coma* (London: Flamingo, 1998), 213.

4. Don DeLillo, *White Noise* (London: Picador, 1985), 51.

Chapter 7

1. See James Joyce, *A Portrait of the Artist as a Young Man* (London: Penguin Books, 2000), 3.

Chapter 8

1. William Brennan, *Dehumanizing the Vulnerable: When Word Games Take Lives* (Chicago: Loyola University Press, 1995), 3.

2. George Lakoff and Mark Johnson, *Metaphors We Live By* (Chicago: University of Chicago Press, 1980), 4.

3. Ibid., 5.

Chapter 9

1. Jonathan Franzen quoted in Gordon Burns, "After the Flood," a review in *The Guardian*, November 15, 2003, 6.

2. George Steiner, *Language and Silence: Essays 1958–1966* (Harmondsworth, Middlesex: Penguin Books, 1979), 15.

3. Søren Kierkegaard, *Either/Or: Part I*, edited and translated by Howard V. Hong and Edna H. Hong (Princeton: Princeton University Press, 1987), 127.

Chapter 11

1. Aidan Mathews, *In the Poorer Quarters* (Dublin: Veritas, 2007), 22.

2. Fyodor Dostoevsky, *The Brothers Karamazov*, translated by Constance Garnett, revised by Ralph E. Matlaw (New York: W. W. Norton & Company, 1976), 268.

3. Ibid.

4. Ibid., 277.

5. Ibid., 282.

6. Charles Dickens, *A Tale of Two Cities* (Oxford: Oxford University Press, 1998), 1.

7. Denis Donoghue, *The Sovereign Ghost: Studies in Imagination* (London: Faber & Faber, 1976), 29.

8. Quoted in Manfred Stassen, ed., *Martin Heidegger: Philosophical and Political Writings* (New York: Continuum, 2003), 297.

www.ingramcontent.com/pod-product-compliance
Lightning Source LLC
Chambersburg PA
CBHW021105090426
42738CB00006B/505